South West Coast Path

Exmouth to Poole

Roland Tarr was born and brought up in West Somerset and has close family ties with Exmoor. He was Heritage Coast Officer in Dorset from 1974 to 1988.

D1335368

South West Coast Path

Exmouth to Poole

Roland Tarr

Aurum
in association with

NATURAL
ENGLAND

Acknowledgements

My thanks to the following organisations and people for help and advice: the Devon, Cornwall and Wessex Regional Offices of the National Trust and the National Trust wardens; the highways departments of Devon and Dorset County Councils; the Dorset and East Devon Heritage Coast Services; English Nature local offices; Exmouth Tourist Information Centre; Jo Draper for checking the Dorset historical bits; Sarah Welton for the article on marine wildlife; Norman Barns for helping me find my way through the Axmouth–Lyme Regis Undercliffs.

The author and publishers thank Mark Owen, Trail Officer for the Path, and Alex Green, both of Natural England's South West Coast Path Team, for their help.

This revised and updated edition published in 2011 by Aurum Press,
7 Greenland Street, London NW1 0ND • www.aurumpress.co.uk
in association with Natural England.
www.naturalengland.org.uk • www.nationaltrail.co.uk

Book design by Robert Updegraff
Printed and bound in Italy by Printer Trento Srl

Cover photograph: *Durdle Door (Alamy)*
Title page photograph: *The Cobb, Lyme Regis, at dawn (Alamy)*

Aurum Press want to ensure that these National Trail Guides are always as up to date as possible – but stiles collapse, pubs close and bus services change all the time. If, on walking this path, you discover any important changes of which future walkers need to be aware, do let us know. Either email us on **trailguides@aurumpress.co.uk** with your comments, or if you take the trouble to drop us a line to:
Trail Guides, Aurum Press, 7 Greenland Street, London NW1 0ND,
we'll send you a free guide of your choice as thanks.

Contents

Circular walks appear on pages 43, 44, 66, 120, 134–5, 152–3

How to use this guide

The 630-mile (1008-kilometre) South West Coast Path is covered by four National Trail guides. Each guide describes a section of the path between major estuaries. This book describes the path from Exmouth to Poole, 116 miles (186 kilometres). The guide is in three parts:

• The introduction, historical background to the area and advice for walkers.

• The path itself, described in twelve chapters, with maps opposite each route description. This part of the guide also includes information on places of interest as well as a number of related short walks, starting either from the path itself or at a car park. Key sites are numbered in the text and on the maps to make it easy to follow the route description.

• The last part includes useful information, such as local transport, accommodation, organisations involved with the path, and further reading.

The maps have been prepared by the Ordnance Survey using 1:25 000 Explorer® maps as a base. The line of the Coast Path is shown in yellow, with the status of each section of the Coast Path – footpath or bridleway for example – shown in green underneath (see key on inside front cover). These rights-of-way markings also indicate the precise alignment of the path at the time of the original surveys, but in some cases the yellow line on these maps may show a route which is different from that shown by those older surveys, and in such cases walkers are recommended to follow the yellow route in this guide, which will be the route that is waymarked with the distinctive acorn symbol Q used for all National Trails. Any parts of the path that may be difficult to follow on the ground are clearly highlighted in the route description, and important points to watch for are marked with letters in each chapter, both in the text and on the maps. *Some maps start on a right-hand page and continue on the left-hand page – black arrows (➡) at the edge of the maps indicate the start point.* Should there have been a need to alter the route since publication of this guide for any reason, walkers are advised to follow the waymarks or signs which have been put up on site to indicate this. Since the Coast Path passes through a military exercise area at Chickwell, walkers are advised to pay particular heed to any signs posted and flags flying relating to entry to the area when firing is taking place.

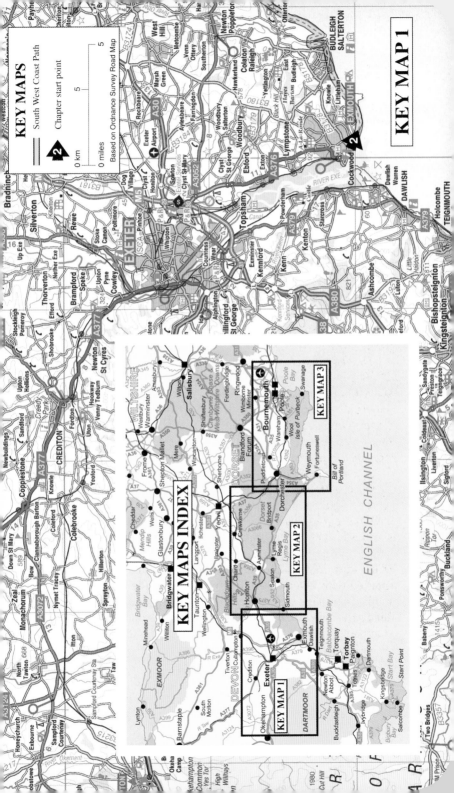

KEY MAPS

— South West Coast Path

▲2 Chapter start point

0 km   5

0 miles   5

Based on Ordnance Survey Road Map

KEY MAP 1

KEY MAPS INDEX

KEY MAP 3

KEY MAP 2

KEY MAP 1

ENGLISH CHANNEL

KEY MAP 2

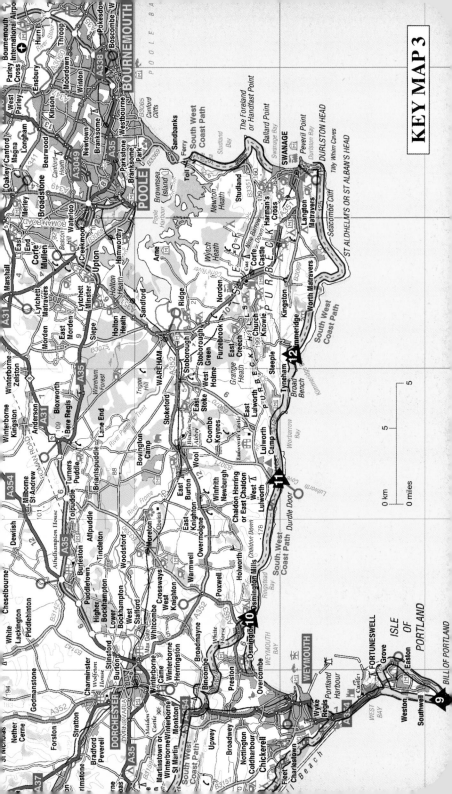

KEY MAP 3

Distance checklist

This list will assist you in calculating the distances between places on the Coast Path where you may be planning to stay overnight, or in checking your progress along the way.

location	approx. distance from previous location	
	miles	km
Exmouth (ferry)	0.0	0
Budleigh Salterton	5.4	8.7
Sidmouth	7.1	11.4
Beer	8.8	14.2
Axe Bridge (for Axmouth)	1.9	3.1
Lyme Regis	6.6	10.6
Charmouth	3.0	4.9
Seatown (for Chideock)	4.0	6.5
West Bay (for Bridport)	3.0	4.9
West Bexington	5.6	9
Abbotsbury (Swannery)	3.7	6
Weymouth (Ferrybridge)	10.9	17.5
Isle of Portland loop		
Portland Bill	5.6	9
Weymouth (Ferrybridge)	7.5	12
Weymouth – Clock Tower	2.7	4.4
Osmington Mills	5.6	9
Lulworth Cove	6.1	9.8
Kimmeridge Bay	7.1	11.5
St Aldhelm's Head (for Worth Matravers)	6.0	9.6
Langton Matravers	2.9	4.7
Swanage (Pier)	4.7	7.5
Old Harry Rocks	3.3	5.3
Studland	1.5	2.4
Poole Harbour (Sandbanks Ferry)	2.7	4.4
location on inland route		
West Bexington	0.0	0
Abbotsbury Castle (for Litton Cheney YHA)	2.1	3.4
Great Hill (for Martinstown)	5.9	9.5
Upwey	2.5	4
Osmington	5.4	8.7
Osmington Mills	1.1	1.7

PREFACE

The South West Coast Path National Trail is a 630-mile (1,008-km) adventure around the coastline of the south-west peninsula. From Minehead on the edge of the Exmoor National Park all the way to the shores of Poole Harbour, the Trail offers every opportunity to enjoy this remarkable coastline, its stunning scenery, rich wildlife and fascinating history.

Between Exmouth and Poole the Trail takes in the entire Jurassic Coast, England's first natural World Heritage Site, with rocks recording 185 million years of the Earth's history. Along this stretch of the Trail you will pass some of Britain's most popular beaches and resorts, as well as busy towns and villages, dramatic cliffs and headlands (such as Beer Head and Old Harry), remote sandy beaches and sheltered coves – some accessible only to people on foot.

The stretch of coast around Weymouth Bay is the first targeted for improvement as part of work to create an All England Coast Path – these changes are scheduled to be ready in time for the sailing events during the 2012 Olympics and Paralympics.

Like other National Trails, this path is waymarked with the distinctive acorn symbol which signals you are on the right route. Whether you plan to stroll out on the cliffs from Sidmouth or Swanage, or walk all the way from Exmouth to Poole, I hope you will enjoy the remarkable beauty of the South West Coast Path.

Poul Christensen CBE
Chair
Natural England

PART ONE

INTRODUCTION

INTRODUCTION

by John Macadam

On the edge of the land

The South West Coast Path must be one of the most spectacular and varied long-distance trails in the world. And at 630 miles (just over 1000 kilometres), from Minehead to Poole, it is certainly Britain's longest. Never far from the sea, the route will take the walker high above the shore and then swoop down to a fishing village in a cove. In fact, someone has calculated that if you walk those 630 miles, you will also climb almost four times the height of Everest! Not that you will need extra oxygen, of course, though windproof insulated clothing can be much appreciated if you are walking into a sou'westerly gale. At other times a T-shirt is more appropriate. But more about that later.

The trail will take you through historic towns and villages, through woods, fields and sand dunes, and alongside quiet creeks and past streams falling from high cliffs into the sea. Occasionally you will walk through a busy town, but often there will be more wildlife – the inevitable gulls, but maybe also seals, basking sharks, dolphins or choughs – than humans. To refresh yourself there are local beers, clotted-cream teas, Cornish pasties, Ruby Red steaks and Dorset Blue cheese, and smoked mackerel. Or you could sample the industrial heritage: pilchard 'palaces' and mining in Cornwall, or quarrying on Portland. If none of that takes your fancy, there are more ethereal pleasures: literary associations, from Daniel Defoe to John Fowles, connections with artists from Turner to Kurt Jackson, the Cornish language ('Kernewek') and innumerable Celtic saints. And if you do not like beer, there's a range of ciders made from traditional varieties of apples in Somerset and Devon, and even a few recently planted vineyards near the Path.

For centuries, local people used paths along the coast for many purposes, including gathering food and looking for wreckage. But in the 18th century the government imposed high import duties on a range of luxury goods, precipitating a rapid growth in smuggling – and yet another use for the paths. The official response was draconian legislation prohibiting anyone from 'lurking, waiting or loitering within five miles from the sea-coast', but the trade was too lucrative to suppress. Finally, in the early 19th century, the coastguard service was set up, with nightly patrols, and so a continuous coast path developed. The coastguards had to be able to look down into coves and narrow inlets, so their route was truly at the edge of the cliffs. But by the early 1800s, a few visitors were using the path for leisure, even if they sometimes had to prove that they had no other purpose!

Use of much of this path was lost, not, as might be expected, by natural geological processes, but by landowners, often backed by the courts, prohibiting access. In 1949 the Act which set up National Parks in England and Wales also set up long-distance paths, including one around the South West Peninsula. The Path was opened in stages, with the last major section opened in 1978, and the patient operation to reinstate the route along the coast is now nearly complete.

Geological processes have indeed destroyed the old coast-guards' tracks in many places, and those same processes are no respecters of hard-won modern routes, so realignment is an ongoing task. Active erosion also means that the geology is exposed in many places, not clothed in soil and vegetation as inland, so the walker will see an impressive range of strata, folds, faults, intrusions, stacks and caves – a real *tour de force*.

Uniquely among the National Trails, the Path passes through two World Heritage Sites: the 95 miles of 'Jurassic Coast' in East Devon and Dorset and the Cornwall and West Devon Mining Landscape. Moreover, the designation of these sites by UNESCO was only the icing on the cake, for much of the Path passes through areas with one or more national designations for land-scape, wildlife or geology: National Park, National Nature Reserve, Heritage Coast, Area of Outstanding Natural Beauty, Site of Special Scientific Interest, and others. But you do not have to be an expert (or understand all these designations!) to enjoy the flow-ers, butterflies and birds you will see at different times of the year.

Management of the Path requires great sensitivity to poten-tially competing interests. Funded primarily by Natural England, this task is shared between approximately 70 staff working for six highway authorities (or their agents), the Ministry of Defence, and the National Trust, and co-ordinated by the South West Coast Path Team based in Exeter. Day-to-day work includes cutting back vegetation, clearing drainage ditches, and replacing broken stiles and signs. In addition to routine maintenance, South West Coast Path managers strive to provide the best experience by realigning sections that involve road walking or re-routing the Path as quickly as possible after cliff-falls have taken place.

Planning your walk

You may be planning to walk the whole length of the Path, or you may just intend to walk a short distance. Even a walk along the promenade is likely to be a walk along the Coast Path! Some of the Path can be enjoyed by people who are less mobile, but very little can be used by cyclists or horse-riders.

If you are planning short walks, there are many circular routes to get you back to your starting point, and in many places there is public transport (but make sure you take the bus or train to your furthest point, then walk back, or else leave yourself plenty of time).

Whatever walk you plan, be sure you are fit enough, particularly if you are planning to walk for several days consecutively. Remember those three Everests! Some people walk the whole Path in one go, and most take 50–60 days to do this. A few people have taken far less time, but they must have missed out a great deal.

The best time to walk the Path is probably May–June, with long days, masses of wild flowers and few people. Another good time is September, when most of the summer visitors have gone. Since the area relies heavily on tourism, there is a wide range of accommodation, from campsites, youth hostels, B&Bs (bed & breakfast) to rather grand hotels, though everywhere can become full at the height of the tourist season in July and August and it is wise to book ahead. If you intend to camp away from a recognised campsite, you will need to ask permission of the landowner, usually the local farmer, and remember to leave no trace of your stay.

If you plan to walk between October and April, you may have the luxury of the Coast Path to yourself. You may also find some ferries are not running and public services, like buses and trains, are running a restricted winter schedule. Tourist Information Centres (TICs), the information section at the back of this book and the National Trail website (www.nationaltrail.co.uk) will either provide the necessary information or give you the necessary contacts.

Equipment

British weather is notorious for its changeability, and the weather in the South West is generally wetter, windier and warmer than most of Britain. Most of the Coast Path is very exposed to the elements; the exceptions are some of the estuaries. The relative exposure depends on which way the wind is coming from – the prevailing wind is southwesterly – and which way the coast faces. The effects of windchill can be extreme: windchill is caused by the wind evaporating moisture from your skin.

With all this in mind, it makes sense to get a weather forecast (from the media, by telephone or the web) and be prepared. It is always sensible to carry a windproof waterproof: the breathable ones are best, and the reproofable ones with a lifetime guarantee are the best of all.

There are various types of walking trousers, though most people use quick-drying polycotton fabrics, with waterproof overtrousers. Denim is decidedly unwise as when wet it becomes stiff and heavy, and is also very slow to dry, thus increasing the risk of hypothermia. A hat of some form is recommended, and a supply of sunscreen to be applied in good time to your neck, arms and anywhere else that is exposed. Traditionally, strong shoes or walking boots with good grips have always been recommended, though some people are very happy wearing sandals designed for walkers.

Finally, walkers need to take an adequate supply of liquid, a whistle and a first-aid kit, all in a rucksack which is adjusted to fit the wearer comfortably. Of course, long-distance walkers will have far more to carry than this, but will take trouble to minimise the weight. Some companies and B&B owners will transport your pack for you to your next stop, for a fee, so that all you need to carry is a daypack. Cash machines are only to be found in the larger towns, so paying bills and withdrawing cash can be a problem, especially for visitors without a sterling cheque account.

Finding your way

The sign for all National Trails is a stylised acorn, and you will find this cut into wooden waymarks, chiselled into stone waymarks, cast in metal, and stuck to aluminium road signs. Most signs also bear the words 'Coast Path'.

You should have few problems following the acorns and thus the trail. The route is also shown on the maps in this guidebook. You may find that the route has changed from that shown on the maps, in which case follow the acorns and any diversion signs. The reason for the latter may well be a cliff-fall, or the Path starting to crumble away. It is obviously foolhardy to ignore diversion signs.

Kimmeridge Bay is famous for its unusual coastal scenery, geology and colourful marine wildlife and is great for surfing, windsurfing, diving, snorkelling and walking. Kimmeridge has given its name to a whole geological classification worldwide. The Purbeck Marine Wildlife Reserve is the longest established Voluntary Marine Nature Reserve in the UK. The Fine Foundation Marine Centre, with its excellent displays and aquaria, provides a really good background to help make a visit to the bay, its ledges and rockpools even more rewarding.

Safety

The main safety message is: keep to the Path. The Path is close to the edge of the cliff in many places. Make sure you are suitably equipped both for your walk and for changing weather conditions.

Those who go down to beaches and rocks beside the sea need to be aware of the tides, with around 9 metres between high and low tide at Minehead, though only a couple of metres at Poole. Every year people get cut off by the tide and have to be rescued. People also get washed off rocks by so-called 'freak waves'. At many places around this coastline you can watch surfers waiting for the bigger waves.

Bathing too can be hazardous, chiefly because of currents. It is best only to swim in safe areas patrolled by lifeguards, who are employed only in the summer. Many beaches have rip currents which drain most of the water that comes onto the beach. If you get caught in a rip current, do not try to swim against it, but rather swim diagonally across it until you are in stiller water, when it is safe to swim back to the beach.

If you do get into difficulties on the Path, the international alarm call is six long blasts on a whistle, followed by one minute's silence.

The coastguards are responsible for dealing with any emergency that occurs on the coast or at sea. Please remember that there are no coastguard lookouts now, and the service relies on the watchful eyes of the public. If you see vessels or people you think are in distress, dial 999 (or 112 on a mobile) and ask for the coastguard. Beneath some cliffs there may be no mobile signal.

The Act forbidding 'lurking, waiting or loitering within five miles from the sea-coast' was repealed in 1825, so relax, explore and enjoy the South West Coast Path and the coasts of Somerset, Devon, Cornwall and Dorset.

The mild winters and warm waters of Poole Harbour allow English avocets to over-winter here. You can also see them in the Exe Estuary.

PART TWO

SOUTH WEST COAST PATH

Exmouth to Poole

1 Crossing the Exe

If you are walking the South Devon section of the South West Coast Path in summer and need to cross the Exe, you can catch the Starcross Ferry which runs an hourly service, seven days a week, from May to October. It leaves Starcross from 10am to 4pm on the hour daily with an additional last ferry at 5pm, May to October, 5.45pm in July and August. It leaves Exmouth for Starcross from 10.30am to 4.30pm on the half hour, with an additional last ferry at 5.30pm May to October, 6.15pm in July and August. The ferry is reached through Starcross Station **1**.

Near the station is the site of Brunel's Atmospheric Pumping Station, a relic of one of the great experiments of 19th-century industrial enterprise. The general idea was literally to vacuum trains along the new line from Exeter to Newton Abbot. The railway actually carried passengers for a whole year in 1847 and speeds of nearly 70mph (112 km/h) were reported before financial problems forced the experiment to cease.

If you are in a hurry and the Starcross Ferry is not running at the time, catch a train into Exeter from Dawlish or Dawlish Warren and then back to Exmouth, using the regular services on both sides of the estuary.

At the time of writing there is an hourly service on weekdays between Dawlish and Exeter St David's **4**. At weekends it is a two-hourly service. Between Exeter St David's and Exmouth there is a half-hourly service on weekdays, a little less frequently on Sundays.

Perhaps the most attractive way to cross the Exe, and certainly the most interesting, is to walk the whole way from Dawlish Warren to Topsham. This is about 6 miles (10 km) of flat walking, half of which is on country lanes. You may prefer to avoid 2 miles (3 km) of walking on roads by catching the train to Starcross **1**.

Then you can visit the historic Powderham Church **2**, enjoy views across the Exe, and possibly see fishermen at work seining. This ancient method of fishing for salmon involves two small boats with a long narrow net stretched between them. Gradually the net is brought round in a circle to enclose a pond-sized stretch of river and, with luck, a large salmon is caught.

You will have time to inspect the ancient Exeter Canal, which was started in 1564, and Topsham is well worth a visit.

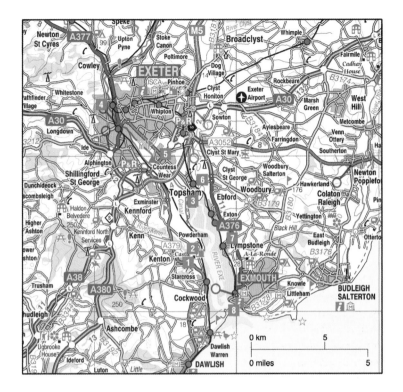

Follow the roads along the western side of the River Exe through Starcross and past Powderham Castle. On reaching Powderham Church **2** on a sharp corner, continue north along a track, cross the railway after 300 yards, and follow the dyke northwards for 1½ miles (2 km). You will eventually come to the seaward end of the Exeter Canal.

The Turf Inn stands by the lockside and sometimes ancient barges are moored there.

The walk north along the west towpath to Topsham takes only half an hour and is very attractive. At Topsham there is a bridge over the canal and a ferry **3** across the Exe which runs every day except Tuesdays, April–September. This can be hailed during the following times: 11am to 5.30pm May–September inclusive, and at weekends only 11am–5.30pm October– April, subject to tides and weather. Lunch break is normally 1pm to 2pm, but may be varied to allow for tides.

The town lies on a tongue of land between the Exe and the Clyst. If you walk south from the ferry you will reach the Strand, with beautiful houses built in the Dutch style by merchants who traded with The Netherlands in past centuries. The houses still have their Dutch-style private courtyards and enclosed gardens. Among these merchants' houses is the museum, Holman House (number 25), open 2pm–5pm Mondays, Wednesdays and Saturdays and most Sundays from June to September, and well worth a visit.

You can continue to the end of the Strand along a footpath/quay, then turn left through the country lanes and cross the railway bridge to get to the ancient bridge crossing the Clyst **6** and the riverside pub. Turn left and you will come to Topsham Station in a couple of minutes. From Topsham to Exmouth there is a half-hourly train service offering good views of the estuary.

A further route via Countess Wear would take you to Starcross and Powderham Church **2**, and along the banks of the Exe to The Turf Inn, following the route just described. You then follow the Exeter Canal all the way to Countess Wear, where you can stay overnight in the youth hostel **5**.

A mile or so before you reach Countess Wear you pass under the M5 motorway and when you get to the A38 turn right by the swing bridge, cross the old bridge over the Exe and take the first turning on the left by the café. The youth hostel **5** is a short way down this road.

To return to the Coast Path at Exmouth you can walk along a riverside public footpath to Topsham from Countess Wear. However, this involves scrambling along the muddy banks of the estuary and the path is flooded at high tide. A new cycle route around the Exe estuary is under construction and will soon change – and improve – the walking route.

I would therefore advise walking back along the Exeter Canal, from the swing bridge at Countess Wear to Topsham, and crossing the Exe by the ferry there **3**. From Topsham you can catch the half-hourly train service to Exmouth.

In the Exe Estuary the RSPB has two nature reserves on areas of coastal grazing marsh that are on opposite sides of the river, not far from the historic city of Exeter. One is at the Exminster Marshes and the other at Bowling Green Marsh near Topsham. In spring lapwings and redshanks and the rare Cetti's warblers can be seen. In winter there are thousands of waterbirds, including black-tailed godwits, wigeons and avocets, best seen at high tide when they congregate closer to dry land and are easier to view.

The Exe Estuary – trade, towns and villages

This area is steeped in history for which much of the evidence can still be seen today. This makes it fascinating to explore.

Exeter and Countess Wear

We know that the Romans regarded Exeter as being of strategic importance since it was served by the Foss Way, and any coastal towns or villages with sea access would have been important at the time for both defence and trade.

If you have followed the paths described above to Countess Wear, with its beautiful old bridge and weir across the Exe, you may already have come across the story of the Countess.

She was the Countess of Devonshire, Isabella de Fortibus, and held considerable power, but the City of Exeter, like most medieval cities, was keen to claim its independence. In 1284 the Countess Isabella sent her bailiff to Exeter fish market to collect tithes, which the mayor refused to pay.

The story goes that in retaliation she commanded the construction of the weir which bears her name in order, she said, to supply water power to a mill. The weir then cut the city off from the sea completely. Exeter could no longer function as a port. The city fought back and won the legal action but the weir is still there to the present day.

Exeter had been a major outlet for the hinterland, with ships setting sail to all parts of the known world. The construction of the weir ensured that Topsham now became the major outlet and for two and a half centuries this state of affairs worked much to the benefit of the merchants of Topsham, causing a sharp decline in the wool trade of Exeter.

Then, in the 16th century, Exeter decided to fight back by constructing a canal beside the Exe Estuary just below Topsham, thus bypassing the weir. This was extended in subsequent centuries and Exeter once again became a thriving port. A map in The Turf Inn shows the different periods of construction.

Topsham

Topsham **6** lies at the confluence of the River Clyst, which lends its name to a number of Devon villages, and the Exe. A fine stone bridge crosses the Clyst by a weir and the ancient and traditional Bridge Inn. Topsham may be the original Roman port referred to in this area. This is not certain, but we do know that a settlement existed by the time of Domesday. After the construction of the weir on the Exe it became not only an important port but also a shipbuilding centre.

This trade still provides employment in Topsham, as you will observe as you walk along the river edge, and activity was particularly lively in the 19th century when a spur was built from the railway station to the docks. As you walk around Topsham you can still see some of the store houses and the Dutch gabled buildings along the Strand. To find out more about the Dutch connection, visit the fascinating museum at number 25.

Lympstone

If, in crossing the estuary by one of the methods described above, you get out of the train at Lympstone 7 and follow the rather narrow footpath alongside the estuary to Exmouth, you will be able to enjoy visiting this attractive village. There are Georgian houses and thatched cottages, and in former centuries boats were also constructed here. At the end of the 19th century a fleet of 100 fishing vessels operated from the village.

Exmouth

Exmouth is now a busy seaside resort with a large beach offering a range of holiday activities. In the past, like other coastal ports, Exmouth was expected to send ships in times of conflict to help defend the nation. From Viking times onwards there are frequent stories of the town being sacked by foreign powers as well as by pirates, but until the 18th century it remained a small town centred on the port.

At the very beginning of the fashion for seaside resorts, seawater baths were constructed and it became fashionable to own a large house with its own stables and a view of the sea. Assembly rooms were built and the town has now had nearly 300 years of providing for visitors. Many famous people took up residence in the town, including Lady Nelson and Lady Byron. This is reflected in a number of fine buildings which can still be seen. Exmouth has a museum, which includes a display on the Exe Estuary's maritime and natural history. It is at Shepherd's Walk, off Exeter Road, near the town-centre shopping precinct.

Topsham merchants closely connected with The Netherlands built their houses in the Dutch style.

2 Exmouth to Sidmouth

via Budleigh Salterton
12½ miles (20.2 km)

Follow the entire length of Exmouth's esplanade. At the eastern end a zig-zag path leads to the top of the cliffs. At the top turn right along the wide gravel track to Orcombe Point. For a bit of variety you can go behind the car park just west of the cliffs after passing the Maer, go briefly into Foxholes Hill, and branch right immediately along a clifftop path which rejoins the official route.

At the Point you will find a 'geoneedle' of Portland stone which has inlaid in it a representative series of stone panels placed in the order in which they were deposited during the last 250 million years. This marks the western boundary of the Dorset and East Devon World Heritage Site, the Jurassic Coast. Later in this chapter there is a brief history of conservation on this coast, leading to the UNESCO declaration of the World Heritage Site.

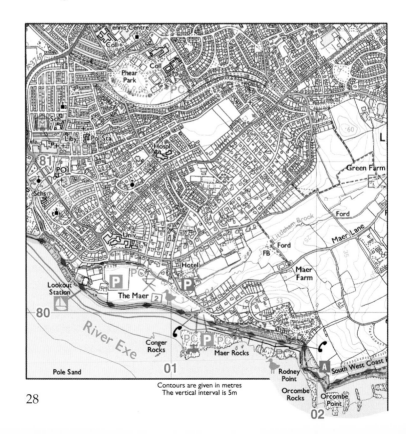

Contours are given in metres
The vertical interval is 5m

There are access points to sandy beaches at Orcombe Rocks (NT) and at Sandy Bay. Here there are facilities including telephones and toilets, a café and a bar which are open during the holiday season. Bus services run to Exmouth from early May until early September.

Next to the large caravan site there is a Royal Marines firing range; keep along the cliff top through the caravan site and then go diagonally across the car park until you come to the fence which marks the boundary of the firing range, then turn left and follow the fence, keeping the firing range on the seaward side. Shortly after passing the firing range entrance on your right, continue along the range boundary, turn left again and cross a large open meadow, which is part of the caravan site, to rejoin the clifftop path as it rises.

To the east of the caravan site the path climbs, dropping only briefly through a tiny wooded valley before rising to the heights of 'The Floors'. At West Down Beacon there is a trig. point beside the path and one or two seats. From this point there is a fairly gentle descent, keeping to the cliff top alongside

Contours are given in metres
The vertical interval is 5m

the East Devon Golf Club then through woodland and over wide lawns down to the Marine Parade at Budleigh Salterton.

This quiet resort, with Georgian, Victorian and Edwardian houses fronting the sea, is pleasant and relaxing. Shops and pubs should be able to supply your needs and the Tourist Information Centre (TIC) can help with accommodation. (If closed, a list of accommodation addresses can be found on the door.)

Now follow the road and then the path along the crest of the beach. When you come into sight of the Otter estuary, go to the far corner of the large car park beside it and then walk ³/₄ mile (1.2 km) north beside the River Otter on a dyke built by Napoleonic prisoners of war. Cross the Otter, go straight ahead along the path just inside the next field and return to the sea along the bank opposite. Note the nature reserve of the Devon Wildlife Trust. To the right there is a hide constructed by the East Devon Countryside Service.

Continue along the cliff top towards Ladram Bay. Just before Ladram there is a kissing-gate and the path cuts across the next field, making for another kissing-gate at the eastern end, and a footbridge. It continues across the next field until it comes to the small lane. This leads down to Ladram Bay with its shingle beach, red sandstone stacks and small caves.

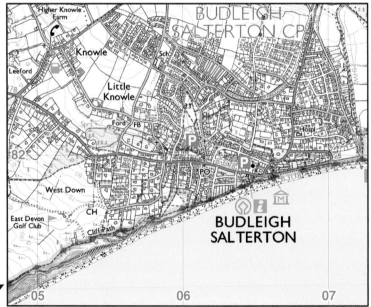

Contours are given in metres
The vertical interval is 5m

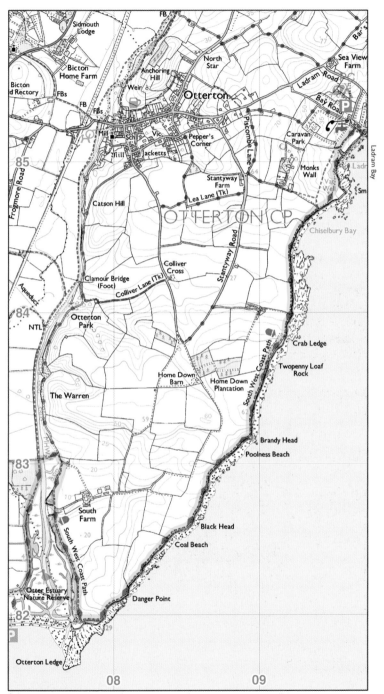

Contours are given in metres
The vertical interval is 5m

31

During the summer season basic facilities are present at the Bay, including a telephone, café and shop. Heading eastwards, go towards the beach a few yards and then left to the seaward side of the mock-Gothic thatched cottage. The path stays on top of the cliff until it enters a plantation in which lies the Iron Age hill fort of High Peak.

Follow the well-defined tracks through the woods just inland of High Peak and continue through fields along the cliff top to Peak Hill. Then go down through the woods, branching right at the junction before turning inland along a garden fence. Steps lead on to the road into Sidmouth behind a thatched house. Follow the road down on the right-hand side for a few yards until you come to the old road, which was closed to traffic in 1997, following a cliff-fall. Pass beside a gate and walk down

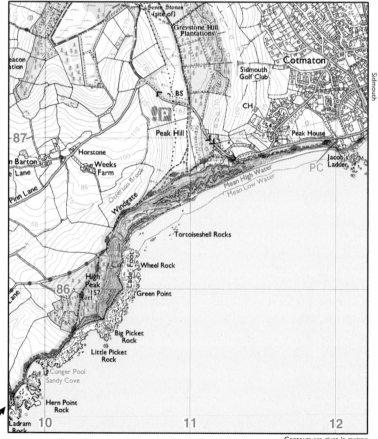

Contours are given in metres
The vertical interval is 5m

The sea front at Sidmouth, a popular resort since the early 19th century.

the old road, through a gate at the lower end and into the lawns which lead down to Jacob's Ladder. There is an award-winning park on your right, with an intriguing restored Second World War pill box near the entrance. To continue east, follow the new Millennium Walkway, which runs from Connaught Gardens across the beach to the Esplanade.

Sidmouth is a fine, restful seaside resort, which has succeeded in combining traditional charms with all the ingredients for a pleasant stay and little to disturb the passing walker. There are good views of the red cliffs of Peak Hill and Ladram to the west as you walk along the sea front. The fishermen sell some of their fresh catch just round the corner from their boats, which are tied up at the eastern end of the beach.

Conserving the Dorset and East Devon World Heritage Site

The Coast Path was formally designated by the Countryside Agency (now Natural England) with the blessing of the government. The path is managed by Devon and Dorset County Councils and the National Trust with government financial support.

Much of the countryside through which the path runs has been formally designated an Area of Outstanding Natural Beauty, which gives national recognition to the high quality of the landscape. Now the whole of the rural coast between Orcombe Point at Exmouth and Old Harry Rocks at Studland has been designated a World Heritage Site.

Heritage Coasts and World Heritage Site status

The idea of special measures for protecting the rural coast became a matter of some urgency just before the Second World War, when the ever-quickening pace of development was already beginning to destroy the beauty of parts of Britain's rural coastline. It was more than twenty years before the government set in motion an official review. In 1970 the Countryside Commission (now Natural England) reported back with a major proposal that 'the most scenically outstanding stretches of undeveloped coast be defined and protected as Heritage Coasts'.

Much of the coast of Dorset and Devon was defined as Heritage Coast by the Commission in association with the local authorities, thus affording it special protection through planning with a strong emphasis on practical action. Heritage Coast teams were set up to work with parish councils, landowners, farmers, voluntary organisations and individuals to co-ordinate a wide range of conservation and recreation tasks and to help in the management of the South West Coast Path to ensure that the conservation of the coastal environment was looked after.

Almost all of the coast in East Devon and Dorset also lies within Areas of Outstanding Natural Beauty (AONBs), which receive special protection and management both to conserve and to enhance the natural beauty of these nationally important landscapes. Some of the organisations which have played a central part in conserving this coast are recorded in the next few paragraphs.

The National Trust (NT) launched its operation 'Enterprise Neptune', now renamed the 'Neptune Coastline Campaign', in 1965 with the aim of acquiring as much as possible of the most

Red squirrels, the only squirrel native to the British Isles, are almost extinct on southern England's mainland but can be seen on Brownsea Island in Poole Harbour.

beautiful stretches of coastline in England and Wales. The Trust made further appeals and now owns 20% of the rural Jurassic Coast. The National Trust's efforts are complementary to those of the East Devon Countryside Service and Dorset Countryside. The latter work with all the owners and occupiers, while the National Trust operation gives the added protection that only ownership can ensure.

Natural England has designated Sites of Special Scientific Interest (SSSIs), with strict guidelines being laid down for their protection. Virtually the whole of this coast is designated as SSSI, primarily for its geological interest, but in addition for the accompanying flora and fauna. Natural England has also been responsible for managing National Nature Reserves (NNRs). You will pass two major ones, at the Undercliffs between Axmouth and Lyme Regis, and at Studland.

The Devon and Dorset Wildlife Trusts manage numerous reserves along the path which are mentioned in the route description. Both these organisations also give much help and advice to those who are involved in the day-to-day management of this coastline.

The British Trust for Conservation Volunteers (BTCV), and its affiliated local voluntary groups in each county, have carried out much of the practical conservation work on these coasts over the past 30 years.

A fossil fish from the Jurassic period, **Dapedium politum**, *found at Lyme Regis.*

The Royal Society for the Protection of Birds (RSPB) manages the reserves at Exminster and Topsham, near the start of this walk, at Radipole and Lodmoor at Weymouth, and the Arne reserve near the finishing point at Poole Harbour.

World Heritage Site status 2001

After five years of diligent activity, 1995–2000, an application was made to the United Nations Educational, Scientific and Cultural Organisation (UNESCO) in July 2000. After a site inspection there was a meeting in Helsinki in December 2001 at which the Dorset and East Devon World Heritage Site, also known as the Jurassic Coast, was designated. It is the first and sole natural World Heritage Site in England. The nearest such site is the Giant's Causeway and St Kilda and it joins such world-famous natural sites as the Great Barrier Reef, the Rhine Valley and the Grand Canyon. In other categories are the Taj Mahal and the Pyramids.

Among the UNESCO criteria for such a qualification are 'that the site should be an outstanding example, representing major stages of the earth's history including the record of life, significant ongoing geological processes in the development of landforms, or significant geomorphic and physiographic features; and that the site should contain superlative natural phenomena or areas of exceptional natural beauty and aesthetic importance'.

As you walk along this coast from Orcombe to Old Harry Rocks at Studland you will see that this is the most varied and beautiful coast. That 'significant geological processes' are still taking place will become evident where major erosion is taking place. It has been called the Jurassic Coast because of the dinosaur-bearing strata, although the rocks represented extend to both sides of this period.

The Dorset and East Devon Coast is thus recognised as being globally important for the earth sciences. The coast is special because it represents 185 million years of the Earth's history in just 95 miles (160 km) of coastline. Walk the coast and take a walk through time; discovering the geological story for yourself. The site runs from Exmouth to Studland and contains a complete record through the Triassic, Jurassic and Cretaceous periods of geological time. The oldest rocks are an incredible 250 million years old.

See the bibliography at the end of the book for further reading on the World Heritage Site you are just about to walk.

3 Sidmouth to Beer

through Branscombe
8½ miles (14 km)

Leaving Sidmouth, cross the River Sid on the ornate Alma footbridge at the eastern end of the beach. Go inland and uphill and then turn right into Cliff Road, parallel with the cliffs. Bearing sharp left at the end, the lane then turns right going past the landward side of the former coastguard cottages (Laskeys Lane). Turn right towards the cliffs to the left of The Rocket House and left along the cliffs to Salcombe Hill. Salcombe Hill is a good viewpoint with easy access from a car park. At the edge of the plateau there is a direction finder and viewpoint **9**.

In the next valley is Salcombe Mouth, a secluded shingle beach accessible by a steep path. Beer Head comes into sight and the yellow stripe of greensand (it is green when first exposed) identifies Higher Dunscombe Cliff.

At Salcombe Mouth cross the stream by the footbridge just back from the cliff and climb to Dunscombe Cliff. After reach-

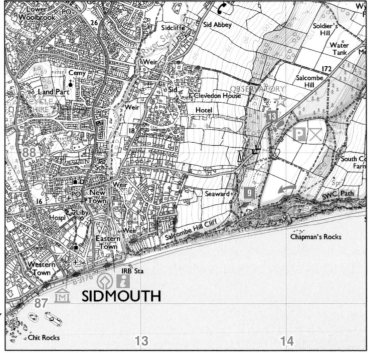

Contours are given in metres
The vertical interval is 5m

ing the kissing-gate at the top, cross several level fields up to a stile at the eastern end of the plateau, where you come into sight of the Lincombe Valley. Pass to the landward side of this wild and overgrown hollow, keeping more or less on the level. About 400 yards (365 metres) inland drop down to a stile to rise briefly on the other side and regain your original height.

The path meanders through many old lime pits **10** before coming close to the edge of Lower Dunscombe Cliff. A zig-zag path through Dunscombe Coppice and the meadow below then connects the cliff top and Weston Mouth.

Weston Combe is a valley of hedgerows, small fields and wild flowers. Weston Mouth has a shingle beach with a few weathered chalets nestling among the windswept undergrowth. The path descends to the beach briefly before rising back up a gully to the low cliff top, which, on both sides of the valley, is owned by the National Trust. A climb to the east brings the path to the top of Weston Cliff.

The path stays near Weston Cliff for the length of two very large fields and then strikes diagonally across the next field. It

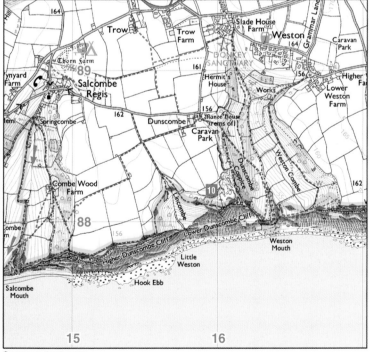

Contours are given in metres
The vertical interval is 5m

then crosses a small hanging valley, Littlecombe Hollow, and goes over a stile. Go back to the clifftop slopes, through several fields, cross another stile and you will see a low, stony bank, the western rampart of Berry Cliff Camp (see 'Pre-Roman times on the coast', page 120). After another 500 yards (450 metres) cross the easternmost bank and descend into an area of overgrown woodland which has colonised the old chalk pits behind Branscombe **11** (see page 44 for a circular walk in this area). Go left on to the well-defined track which keeps parallel with the cliffs.

Continue directly eastwards where the route enters National Trust property. A junction branching sharp left allows you to descend to the fascinating village church and, further on, a working smithy **14**, a café in the former village bakery, and the village mill **12**. A clearly marked footpath will return you back down beside the stream to Branscombe Mouth. You could also make a detour to The Masons Arms

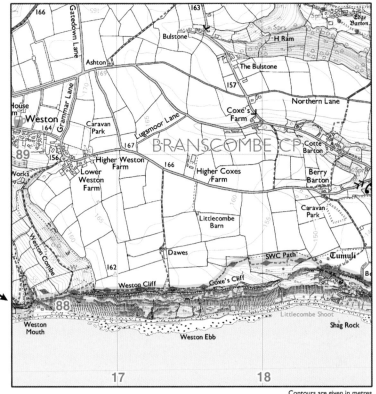

Contours are given in metres
The vertical interval is 5m

higher up the road. However the Coast Path continues straight on parallel to the cliffs.

Nearing Branscombe Mouth, keep just inland of the former coastguard cottages. At Branscombe Mouth there is a café, shop and car park next to the popular shingle beach.

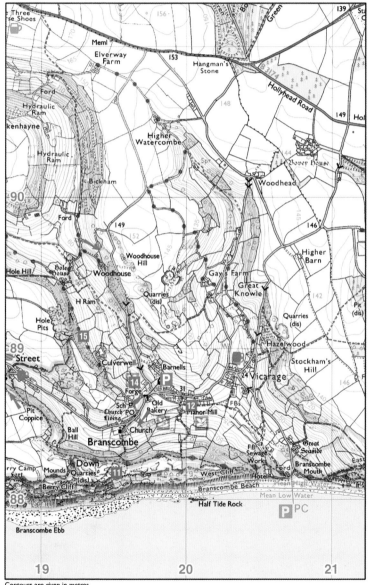

Contours are given in metres
The vertical interval is 5m

From here, to go towards Beer you cross a small footbridge and one field. You then have a choice. You can either follow the official route down into the spectacular Under Hooken and climb out of the eastern end, or you can keep to the cliff top until the paths reunite. Now the route hugs the cliff and finally goes across to join a small lane which runs along the seaward edge of a caravan site, and down the road to the fishing village of Beer.

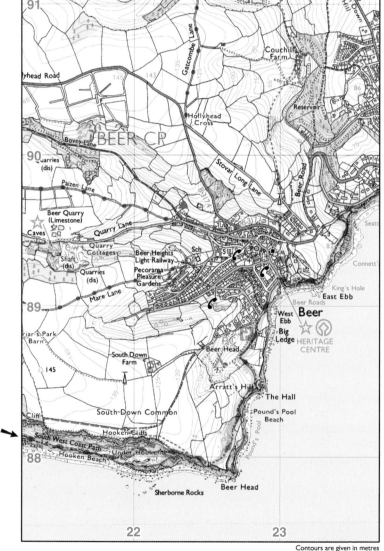

Contours are given in metres
The vertical interval is 5m

A CIRCULAR WALK AT SALCOMBE HILL

2½ miles (3.9 km) (see maps on pages 38–39)

To reach Salcombe Hill car park **13**, where the walk starts, leave the Lyme Regis–Exeter A3052 road at the signs for Salcombe Regis. Keep to the road markings and follow signs for Sidmouth, passing north of Thorn Farm, formerly the seat of the Manor Court, and the Salcombe Thorn, carefully preserved by the village since the welfare of the community is believed to depend on its health. Just over ¹/₂ mile (0.8 km) past the Salcombe Thorn you will see the car park.

At the back of the car park you will see a waymarked route leading south. Follow this and take the first left turning from it. Go straight on at each of the junctions and soon you will come into sight of thatched buildings across the valley to the right. Keep going and you will soon see the church of St Peter and St Mary and the village of Salcombe Regis straight ahead up the wooded valley. On reaching the village continue up the lane to Salcombe Church, which has many 15th-century features.

For Salcombe Mouth come out of the church and retrace your steps down the hill, but keep to the surfaced lane until just before the road branches slightly left for Coombe Wood Farm.

Turn right here through a kissing-gate and almost straight away leave the field track to go through a second kissing-gate to continue down the side of the valley, keeping the hedge to your left. The narrow path goes straight ahead through a meadow and small field and then turns left into the valley bottom by a farm shed. Now follow the stream down to the sea at Salcombe Mouth. There are steep steps leading down to a secluded shingle beach. To continue, turn westwards towards Sidmouth along the Coast Path. During the steep climb west you may see bluebells, speedwell and red campion in the spring.

At the top of a flight of steps there is a junction with a path leading inland. Carry straight on along the Coast Path through a wide bridlegate and past the South Coombe Farm memorial stone. From the National Trust donations cairn and a direction finder follow the wide, flat, grassy path back inland to the Salcombe Hill car park.

Route to Salcombe Hill cliff for elderly or infirm people: park in the same place as for the previous walk but, instead of following the directions above to Salcombe Regis, follow Southdown Drive and keep going seawards all the way to the cliff top, and return by retracing your steps.

A CIRCULAR WALK AT BRANSCOMBE
2½ miles (4.2 km) (see map on page 41)

Park at the village hall car park **14**, turn right and follow the road up towards the church. After about 100 yards you will come to the village post office and the 16th-century 'Church Living' on your right, with the church on your left. Much of the structure is Norman. There is a 15th-century wagon roof and the screen, gallery and altar rails are all Jacobean. The 18th-century pulpit has three tiers. There are several fine memorials, one of which commemorates the Wadham family who lived just up the road at Edge Barton and founded Wadham College, Oxford.

Coming out of the church door go straight ahead through the churchyard and across the valley into the woods. Steps lead up through the woods and, shortly after climbing a stile near the top, you come to a well-defined track. Turn right (west) and continue along this wooded track until you see an open meadow on the northern, landward side, with a farm track leading across the middle.

Follow this farm track inland and bear left to keep the woodland ahead to your right. At the end of the second field the path enters the woods and descends diagonally to Street, with The Fountain Head pub and a group of cottages. Make your way past the pub and facing you at the end of the lane is a gateway with a track rising steeply through it towards the right. After passing several chalk outcrops and rising into a meadow at the top, bear left towards the woods ahead and enter them through a bridlegate.

Go diagonally left across the copper ore pits **15** and follow the track at the far side north and inland for about 110 yards. Here fork right off the track on to a path down through the woods which will bring you into a narrow lane. Keep going inland on the same side of the valley to Hole House.

Turn down in front of the house to the bottom of the valley. After crossing the stream keep on up the lane, which bends slightly right, and then take the hairpin bend backwards to return down the valley. Continue past Woodhouse Farm to join the lane, which will shortly take you back to the village hall.

Branscombe village was once the scene of a considerable cottage industry, based on the wool trade.

The wool trade

All the way along this path there are small villages apparently with no great source of wealth or industry. Yet beautifully decorated parish churches or substantially built stately homes of other centuries are evidence of past wealth.

From early medieval times, the hinterland of this coast was found to be an excellent place for agriculture in general and in particular for the breeding of sheep for wool. Most of the agricultural products of the hinterland would have been used for home consumption, but a number of developments in the wool trade led to a thriving export industry which was to bring great wealth to the coastal ports of Dorset and East Devon.

Edward III did much to encourage the spinning and weaving of cloth when he forbade the export of raw wool. As time went on, the immigration of Flemish weavers and the French Huguenots helped to develop cloth manufacture of a high quality.

In the beginning the industry would have been supplied with enough sheep locally to enable the manufacturers to have extremely low raw material costs. The great abbeys, which owned large tracts of land along the route covered by this path, notably Glastonbury, Bindon, Forde, Sherborne and Abbotsbury, would have derived much of their income from their agricultural estates. The evidence of their wealth can still

Cliffs near Sidmouth.

be seen, particularly at Abbotsbury through which the Coast Path passes.

Initially the spinning and weaving was an urban industry, with the countryside merely supplying the wool. However, at some time around 1400 the industry began to take over rural sites, where there was water power, previously used only for grinding corn.

Many of these medieval mills have left traces or are even standing today. A recent study showed that in Dorset every mill which can still be traced was already in action at the time of Domesday in 1086.

The old method of treating wool cloth was to tread on the cloth in a tank of water, and this demanded relatively little water. The treatment of cloth by the new method of 'fulling' (treating the cloth mechanically) needed mechanical power, so many mills were converted to the new, more lucrative, work. Traditionally, the villagers would have made cloth in their cottages and probably sold any surpluses in the towns. Thus it was not difficult for the new mill owners to find skilled labour out in the country.

Cottage industry would have been a feature of nearly all the villages through which the Coast Path passes, but often there is little evidence of it in the architecture. However, at Branscombe you may notice three-storey cottages near the old mill. They are often an indication of the weaving industry, with looms being located on the top floor for extra light.

The industry would have had its ups and downs from the medieval period until the early 19th century, and one mill might have changed its trade from cloth to corn several times according to the prevailing economics. With the huge increase in trade in the 19th century, however, the small streams and rivers that served the mills near this coast were no longer able to supply enough power to meet the growing demand. Gradually the cloth industry moved away to the north, where steam power from coal was almost limitless.

Hand-made Dorset buttons

This great cottage industry of the 18th and early 19th centuries employed many women and children, and two coastal villages which obtained a reputation for their buttons were Wool and Langton Matravers. The collapse of the Dorset button trade from the mid-19th century was caused by the rise of button-making in the industrial Midlands.

Seaton Hole: Seaton Bay on the Devon Jurassic Coast is where the red cliffs of the Triassic period meet the chalk cliffs of the Cretaceous period due to a geological fault which has raised the red cliffs upwards out of their time frame. The summer sun has allowed the seaweed to bloom and strong tides have exposed the red mudstone rocks.

4 Beer to Lyme Regis

over Axe Bridge and past Culverhole Point
8½ miles (13.6 km)

Above the beach and opposite The Anchor Inn in Beer follow
the surfaced path which starts on a more or less level course
and then rises through gardens to the cliff top up a set of stone
and concrete steps overlooking the fishing boats pulled up on
the pebbles. There is also an alternative signed route avoiding
the steep steps. Keep to the cliff top for 400 yards (360 metres).
The path leads into a narrow lane. Turn sharp right down this
to a post box and telephone kiosk by Seaton Hole. At low tide
you can go down the steep path and walk along the beach to
the sea-front path at the Chine. Otherwise follow the clifftop
road east and keep straight on for about 600 yards (540 metres)
to the far end of a large terrace of houses on the right. Near the
end is a footpath sign pointing towards the sea. Follow this,
turn left at the sea front and continue to the bridge at Axmouth.

Axmouth, two-thirds of a mile (1 km) upstream from the
bridge and harbour, is a pleasant old village with thatched cottages, two inns and accommodation; the church is worth a detour.
There is tent camping at Axe Farm, in the field right opposite.

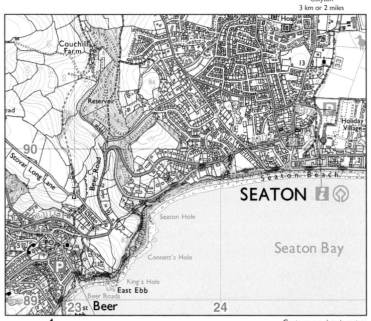

Contours are given in metres
The vertical interval is 5m

The wharf at Axmouth, which is an attractive village well worth a detour.

Note that the old bridge over the Axe **16**, still standing beside the new one, is one of the earliest concrete bridges still surviving, built in 1877 but disguised as a masonry bridge.

Just north of the bridge is a sign, 'Welcome to Axe Bridge Golf Club'. The Coast Path follows the lane past the old coastguard cottages and passes to the landward side of the club house. Through the golf course keep straight up the valley until you come to a narrow track, with views back towards Beer Head, the westernmost chalk cliffs of the south coast.

Two hundred yards up this lane, opposite a stile for the path to Axmouth village, the Coast Path turns off right (south), as a narrow grassy track between hedges. In the next fields follow the hedge seawards to a gap where you go left diagonally across the field (south east). The path stays above the reserve and then descends into the Undercliff National Nature Reserve at the entrance point, which is clearly indicated, beside a bench and Coast Path sign. I am now going to describe the path as it was in 2003; you may find that it has changed in part since then because of further landslips. The wardens keep a route waymarked through the area, so always follow their signs rather than adhering slavishly to this guide (see page 58 for further information about the reserve).

Remember that once you enter the reserve it is over 6 miles (10 km) to the other end. Some of this walking can be demanding, particularly if it has rained recently and the paths are slippery on the steeper slopes. The only way out is to retrace your steps or to continue to Lyme Regis. There are no public access points along the way.

The path passes through almost jungle-like woodland for the whole way, but from time to time magnificent views will open up through gaps in the trees. If you walk quietly you may see some roe deer, badgers and foxes.

Not far to the east of the reserve entrance the path follows the ridge of a natural bank, with a chasm to the landward side, which probably formed about 200 years ago.

This bank is the result of a classic rotational slip, where the weight of the descending rock and soil on the landward side has actually pushed this great mound of material upwards.

A little further east again the path emerges to give one last glimpse of Beer Head before diving back into the undergrowth.

When a clear view of the sea next opens out you will see the cliff face of 'Goat Island' **17** (see page 58). The area below this is called Culverhole Gully, and there were once plans to establish

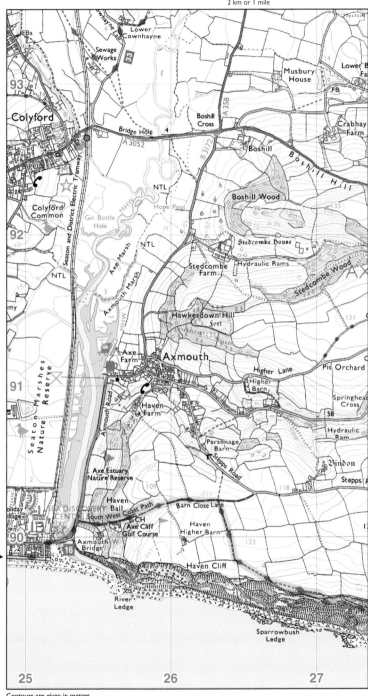

Contours are given in metres
The vertical interval is 5m

a harbour here. Just to the east is Culverhole Point. The path again dives into the undergrowth and below the ash trees with their abundance of ivy and the rope-like lianas of traveller's joy. Hart's tongue fern is abundant and in spring red campion provides spots of colour in the dense, dark green undergrowth. The sun filters through only in the clearings and the sky is seen in glimpses through the quivering ash leaves above.

Soon you will find that the path to the east of this winds up and down for a short way before coming on to another ridge, through what could almost be an avenue of sycamore trees. There are similar ridges on either side as far as you can see through the dense undergrowth. The way then enters a small opening and begins to go up and down again. Privet and wood spurge, stinking iris, dog's mercury and the hart's tongue fern are among the multitude of plants that you will see covering the ground.

After about 10 minutes' walk to the east you may notice clearings created by the reserve wardens to diversify the habitat. This was once the garden of Critchard's Cottage, abandoned in the 1839 landslip. The hazel you see growing around here is what remains of hazel coppicing, carried on at the Undercliff until the 1950s.

Just to the east you may notice the ruins of Cliff Cottage, which replaced Critchard's and was lived in until 1950 by the Gappers. Annie Gapper used to serve cream teas to visitors in this delightful setting **18**.

Half an hour's walk east from here you will find a National Nature Reserve information sign **19** and map, where

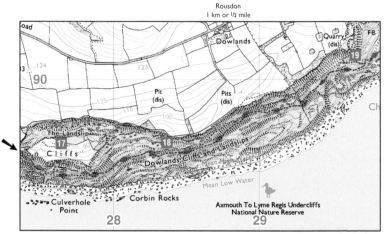

a private track comes down from the landward side. This is roughly the halfway point.

The path follows the track over the bridge and soon branches off seawards to mount a flight of wooden steps upwards through a tunnel of hawthorn and hazel coppice, to emerge on a small peak with a bench **20** overlooking Charton Bay, long ago a favourite landing place for smugglers, with Humble Point just to the east.

The route east of Whitlands Cliff is narrow and clings to the side of a steep slope overlooking a chasm full of bracken.

Once again the path emerges on to a ridge with a small chasm below and 100-foot- (30-metre)-high cliffs topped by a yellow outcrop of greensand above.

If you see a concrete block inscribed 'CR' (Combpyne Rousden is the name of the parish), you are approaching Whitlands Cliff. The path is now well back from the sea and occasionally you will catch glimpses over the enormous 1840 landslip, with Humble Green culminating in Humble Rocks and Humble Point below.

The path now meanders up and down the relatively old and stable-looking landslips. Just east of this you will see holm oak and beech trees, as well as turkey oak and sycamore. Soon the path drops down to Pinhay Springs and from here follow the tarmac track heading east. Climb steadily east for well over a quarter of a mile. After the same distance again the tarmac ends and the Coast Path forks seawards. After the junction the path crosses a small rivulet and a massive four-year-old rotational landslip.

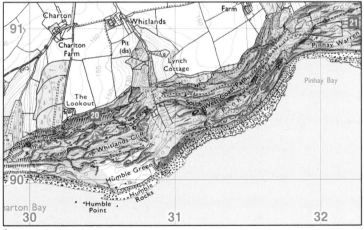

Contours are given in metres
The vertical interval is 5m

You will see another area of great turmoil where the trees lie twisted and broken like matchsticks all the way down to the sea **21**. You will also see ponds typical of those which often form between the banks of rotational slips. These make the area even more unstable, as the water held in them seeps into the soil and helps to cause the next slip.

About 10 minutes' walk to the east of all this you reach the nature reserve boundary sign. Follow the small lane east and parallel to the coast, then branch right at a bungalow onto a gravel path. After a few yards you are at the kissing-gate, the boundary between Devon and Dorset.

To the east of the county boundary the path crosses open meadows (NT). Branch right where the path divides as you come into sight of the houses, and cross a small stream. Branch right again after the stream and you will come to a stile with steps down through the wood that emerge at the bowling green beside The Cobb, the harbour of Lyme.

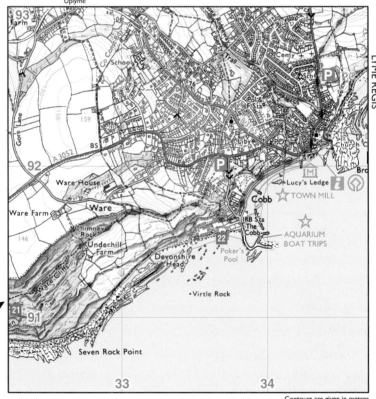

Contours are given in metres
The vertical interval is 5m

The Lyme Regis Museum has first-class displays and will bring to life the history of the town and the area you have just passed through.

The Cobb, of medieval origin, has witnessed many dramas of English history. The most famous was perhaps the support given by Lyme to the defeat of the Armada as it appeared off this coast one day in 1588. In the same century the man who discovered the Bahamas, Sir George Somers, was born in Lyme.

In 1644 The Cobb again played a vital role when Royalist troops besieged the town from the land. Lyme continued to be supplied from the sea and successfully saw off the Royalists. The Restoration of the monarchy in 1660 was therefore not welcome in this town. Religious services had to be held illegally in the surrounding countryside, including on the cliffs above what is now the National Nature Reserve, and when the Duke of Monmouth arrived (near Monmouth Beach **22**) 25 years later he was welcomed and proclaimed king here, and gathered many supporters armed with pitchforks. The savage repression of this rebellion was one of the factors in the success of the Dutch Protestant William of Orange, when three years later he landed in Britain further along the South West Coast Path at Torbay and became king.

The Axmouth–Lyme Regis Undercliffs National Nature Reserve

The 324-hectare reserve was set up by the Nature Conservancy Council (now Natural England) in 1955–56 and contains one of the largest and best examples of land slipping in the British Isles.

In very simplified terms, there are three layers of rocks and soils here. Chalk layers 100 feet high sit on top of greensand, and these two let water through, with a waterproof base of clays which slopes slightly towards the sea.

When it rains two events occur. The upper layers get waterlogged, their many thousands of tons of dry weight become millions of tons, and the wet clay becomes quite slippery. Thus the material above starts sliding, in this case seawards, producing the landscape you now see.

A particularly well-reported case of this slipping, which is an almost constant process, occurred at Christmas 1839. The people who lived and worked there at the time thought it was an earthquake, so dramatic was the sudden movement, and contemporary accounts and melodramatic drawings are on display in the Lyme Regis museum.

Dorset's Jurassic Coast, Axmouth–Lyme Regis Undercliffs National Nature Reserve. The white chalk exposure is caused by the dramatic land movements described on page 57.

One notable feature of this slip, which is at the far Axebridge end of the reserve, is that a large block of land was completely isolated from its neighbouring fields and yet retained its level top, complete with a crop of wheat and turnips, divided from firm land by a dramatic chasm. This became something of a tourist attraction at the time and Queen Victoria came to observe the scene from her Royal Yacht. The chasm is ³/₄ mile (1.2 km) long, and 200 feet (60 metres) deep. The area still remains, called 'Goat Island' **17**, and is now part of the reserve.

Lyme Regis and the surrounding countryside

Those who have read Jane Austen will recognise features of the harbour and the small town huddled on the cliffs opposite, which she described in *Persuasion*.

I recommend a visit to the museum and the 15th-century Parish Church of St Michael the Archangel, which has a number of 12th- and 13th-century features, a mixture which gives the interior a most intriguing and unusual appearance.

The Cobb was probably first built as a wooden structure in the 13th century, and for several centuries Lyme Regis was an important and prosperous outlet for the wool trade of the rich towns of Somerset. In the 17th century there was even trade with the American colonies and the West Indies.

In the middle of the 18th century, however, the economy of this area was at a low ebb and one ship a month was leaving for America with emigrants. Things picked up later and the harbour records show that 600 ships a year used the port during the early 19th century, and that nearly 40 of the ships operated from Lyme. During the Napoleonic Wars, regular fortnightly sailings to the Channel Islands were instituted. In 1830 Lyme had been made a bonding port, and just behind The Cobb the Custom House sits alongside other contemporary warehouses. Shipbuilding also thrived here well into the 19th century.

The tourist industry also came to the rescue and, with the help of Jane Austen and other more recent writers, and now the presence of the ever popular Coast Path, the holiday trade has been providing local people with a livelihood ever since. Although The Cobb attracts little commercial trade these days, it still helps to protect Lyme from erosion and provides a safe haven for fishing and sailing boats.

5 Lyme Regis to West Bay

through Charmouth and Seatown
10 miles (16 km)

The route along the cliff top to Charmouth, giving some of the most stunning views of the whole of this coast, has been closed for some years due to coastal land slips. Negotiations to achieve an off-road route as close to the sea as possible have been proceeding, but at present the alternative route detailed here more or less follows the busy main road the whole way, apart from a brief detour through some fields and a wood, and a shortcut across the golf course. Walkers may prefer to take the bus. Please refer to www.nationaltrail.co.uk for up-to-date information.

Otherwise, from the bridge by the museum pass the traffic lights and make for the church. Keep walking up the street and past the Charmouth Road car park **23**. There is no footway and walkers share the bus slip lane and an entry lane for the car park. Opposite the cemetery there is a small lane, with a stile set in the hedge at the entrance of this lane.

The busy town of Lyme Regis, a fashionable resort in the 18th century and still a tourist attraction.

Contours are given in metres
The vertical interval is 5m

From the stile, the Coast Path goes diagonally across three fields until you reach a small lane, bench, stile and kissing-gate, where you have to turn west for a few yards. Then turn north-east once again to go through the beech plantation and up the steps towards Timber Hill (NT).

Proceed eastwards for about 130 yards (120 metres) to the junction with Timber Hill. Turn right (north) and walk along the road, passing the golf club pavilion on your right, to the junction with the A3052. Follow this road northwards for another 110 yards (100 metres), then turn right on to the public footpath that runs across the golf course and through Fern Hill coppice. When you reach the main road (the A3052 again), turn right and proceed to the roundabout. Continue along the A3052 into Charmouth, then turn right on to Higher Sea Lane to rejoin the Coast Path at Charmouth sea front. Once at the beach, you will find the excellent Charmouth Heritage Coast Centre **24** and car park. This centre has a warden/geologist who gives guided walks, and I can heartily recommend a visit. The building is an old cement works and you can still see lime kiln remains behind it.

From the Heritage Centre go upstream through the car park and then cross the footbridge over the River Way. The cliffs ahead leading up to Stonebarrow Hill are world famous for their fossils, and the huge landslips that occurred in 2001 and more recently have been a great bonus for fossil-hunters. More recent slips have taken place, however, and have resulted in the temporary severing of the Coast Path, so *watch out for signs at this point.*

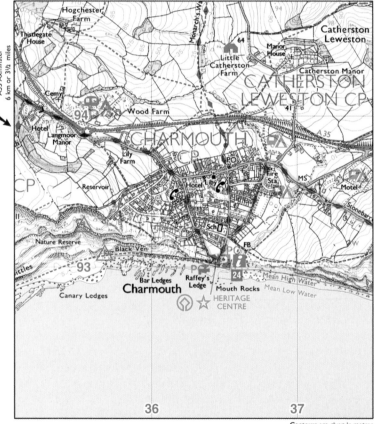

Contours are given in metres
The vertical interval is 5m

If the clifftop path is still deemed unsafe, go up the lane and along a footpath and street to the main road through the village. Turn right and go over the bridge, then go right up Stonebarrow Lane where the main road turns left, turning right again back to the cliff top at Stonebarrow Down.

If you divert inland at Stonebarrow you will find a National Trust shop and information centre and from here you can explore a number of waymarked walks that take you around the Golden Cap Estate.

The Coast Path itself follows the cliff top, continuing to cling to the seaward edge of the fields, down to Westhay Water, up to a stile and then down across the wooded cleft **A** of Ridge Water near the cliff top. Go up again to a stile, keeping the great thorn hedge on your left. Keep to the cliff top, which in places is receding rapidly.

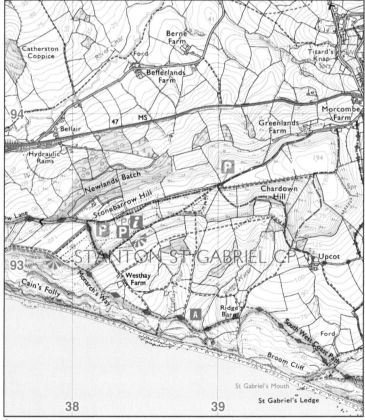

Contours are given in metres
The vertical interval is 5m

Just west of Golden Cap, at 626 feet (190 metres) the highest point on the south coast of England, the path drops into a small hollow, crosses a bridge and then rises across a field to rejoin the cliff top, which it follows until it goes through a kissing-gate giving access to the heather-covered slopes of Golden Cap.

You may like to make a small diversion here, leaving the Coast Path just before the bridge mentioned above, into what was the village of St Gabriel's **25**. Go to the landward side of the cottages in St Gabriel's and up a small trackway towards Golden Cap. There you will see the remains of St Gabriel's Church. In former times the main road, now destroyed by erosion, came through the village of St Gabriel's, which was a thriving community.

Contours are given in metres
The vertical interval is 5m

From the church ruins make straight for the path up the steep slopes of Golden Cap. The path zig-zags up to a small, flat, grassy plateau with a memorial to the past Chairman of the National Trust, the Earl of Antrim, and continues east to the trig. point. Here it goes northwards and inland down the steep slope before branching right (eastwards) once again along a hedgerow. Follow the hedgerow parallel to the cliff top, cross a field immediately south of Langdon Hill, then, just above Seatown, go right through a bridlegate and over a stile into a small wood and across a field. Take the left-hand footpath. When this reaches the road, turn right to walk down to the beach.

From Seatown climb up to Ridge Cliff and pass just behind Doghouse Hill. Then you have the choice of passing behind Thorncombe Beacon or keeping to the cliff top, which is more strenuous but offers magnificent views.

The descent between Thorncombe Beacon and Eype Mouth is straightforward. At Eype Mouth there is a small car park. The village is a quarter of a mile (400 metres) inland with a hotel and inn.

Contours are given in metres
The vertical interval is 5m

Cross Eype Mouth by stepping stones, and stay by the cliff all the way to the top of the hill called West Cliff. The path passes to the landward side of some limestone workings and the ruins of a lime kiln **26**, crosses a field diagonally to the cliff top and then follows the cliff to West Bay. If you wish to visit Bridport **27**, you can simply follow the signs up the Brit River valley and along paths which pass a thatched brewery **28** on the way.

A CIRCULAR WALK AT GOLDEN CAP
2 miles (3 km) (see map on page 64)

The car park on this walk is difficult to find. On the main A35 Bridport–Lyme Regis road there is a short piece of dual carriageway at the top of the steep hill west of Chideock.

At the Chideock end of this dual carriageway a small lane strikes seawards next to a lay-by. Take this lane and a sign will be seen almost immediately, pointing left to the Langdon Hill car park. Park by the information displays and NT donations cairn.

The tracks which go in either direction encircle the forestry of Langdon Hill, so proceed to the seaward end of Langdon Hill immediately behind Golden Cap.

Here you will see a small path leading through a squeezer stile directly towards Golden Cap. Cross the fields and after a short, steep climb to the top of the Cap enjoy the outstanding views.

Retrace your steps back to the track and follow it in the opposite direction to the one from which you came, back to the car park.

This is an easy walk and, with the exception of the last section up Golden Cap, is level, so it can be tackled by people of any age. Glimpses of the old, well-conserved hedgerows of the National Trust property to the west make a fine foreground to the views of Lyme Regis and Devon in the background.

To the east can be seen Thorncombe Beacon, which bears some resemblance to Golden Cap because of its similar geological structure. Beyond that the pier of Bridport Harbour (renamed West Bay by the railway company when it arrived in the 19th century) is quite close. Further off can be seen the wide sweep of the Chesil Bank and the limestone mass of Portland.

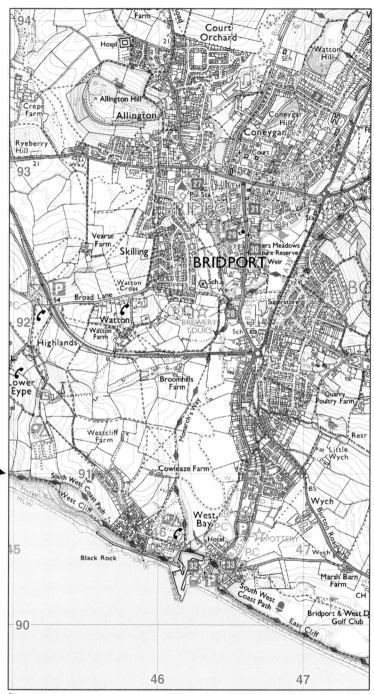

Contours are given in metres
The vertical interval is 5m

67

Bridport town

Bridport is a small rural market town which has retained many of its traditional shop fronts and has not yet been affected by the 'redevelopment' schemes which have destroyed many of the towns of England to the east. It is therefore an ideal place to spend some time.

It was for centuries the home of the rope-making industry and supplied fishing nets to many countries of the world as well as the ropes for shipping.

There are many pubs and tea houses along the main street of the town, and the holiday trade has been an important part of Bridport's economy for 100 years.

In South Street there is the particularly fine medieval parish church of St Mary **29**. A little way south of this are the almshouses and courtyard of the Friends' Meeting House **30**. The almshouses are 15th- and 16th-century town houses with a spiral stone staircase leading out of a courtyard. The story is that the main meeting room was a barn, and that the owner permitted the then illegal Quaker worshippers to meet there in secret. In

The courtyard of the Friends' Meeting House, Bridport.

any event, the owner, Daniel Taylor, gave the Meeting House to the Society of Friends in 1697 and the adjoining buildings were handed over to trustees as almshouses. A visit is recommended.

A hundred yards further south is the 15th-century chantry, possibly an ancient defensive building, and beyond that the thatched brewery with its waterwheel by the River Brit.

In a medieval building near the town centre there is a Bridport Museum **31**, with good displays illustrating many facets of Bridport's fascinating history.

Bridport industries

Ropes for the navy and fishing nets

This industry with its medieval origins was until very recently thriving on the Dorset coast. The fields around Bridport were ideal for growing flax for ropes as early as the 13th century.

Much of the local wealth indicated by the good-quality housing of past centuries, as well as by beautiful churches in Bridport and the villages surrounding it, derived either from the wool trade or from the rope and net industries.

Some of the coastal villages which were involved both with growing hemp and with assistance in the manufacturing process were Eype, Chideock, Burton Bradstock and Abbotsbury. Hemp-growing died out during the 19th century when it became cheaper to buy supplies from Italy and Russia.

About 200 years ago Bridport also started to make sail cloth, and the neighbouring inland town of Beaminster joined in. The flax needed for it continued to be grown by Dorset farmers, and inland at Beaminster the manufacture of sail cloth replaced the local wool trade before the end of the 19th century.

If you look carefully at the small alleyways beside many of the houses in Bridport you will see they have long narrow yards behind them. These are the 'ropewalks', where the ropes used to be made. Imagine the spinning and twisting being carried out in the long gardens, and the various products being hung out in the street to dry.

As rope-making began to take place on a larger scale elsewhere, the town adapted and began to concentrate on the production of nets of all varieties. Up until a few years ago everything from trawler nets to football nets, billiard table pockets and tennis nets were made and exported to all parts of the world. Many of these products were still finished by hand, and so cottage industry was still alive in Bridport and its surrounding villages until the late 1990s.

Man-made fibres, especially nylon, have taken over from natural materials, but Bridport's industries continue to supply high-tech items.

Bridport Harbour

In Saxon and medieval times Bridport's harbour would probably have been quite close to the town centre. As you walk along the Chesil Beach you will notice that the river mouths there tend to get blocked by shingle thrown up by the sea. This must have been a problem in medieval times as well as today. Where there are gaps, these have usually been made by the Environment Agency to allow the water to escape.

In 1721 an Act of Parliament was passed to allow the diversion of the River Brit and the creation of a harbour immediately behind the Chesil Bank. This harbour was completed in 1744 and shipbuilding yards thrived there for nearly 150 years. They had a good reputation for their boats – fishing boats, customs cutters and even naval orders during the Napoleonic Wars. This trade fell into decline in the latter part of the 19th century when iron ships began to replace wooden ones, and the last ship was launched from Bridport in 1879.

The West Dorset District Council is the harbour authority in this area and continues to maintain the port against all the odds. To clear the harbour, the River Brit is dammed with sluices until the valley behind is full of water. The sluices are then opened fully to allow a great surge of water to scour the pebbles from the harbour entrance, a system which has been working now for nearly 250 years.

The Bridport Railway

In 1857 a group of local merchants succeeded in linking Bridport Harbour with the main Dorchester to London railway line. With an eye on the tourist trade, the terminus was called West Bay, and the recently restored railway station **33** still stands just behind the beach, with its cast-iron angle-bracket roof supports embellished with the letters 'BR'. The Company did not have very large funds for this venture and so some of the railway buildings along the route were existing structures rented from local landlords. A row of cottages known as 'Railway Cottages' in one of the villages along the way is clearly many centuries old and the roofs still retain their thatch. The Great Western Railway took over the running of the trains from the outset and the last service ran from Maiden Newton to Bridport in the 1970s.

Bridport Harbour at West Bay, renowned for its shipbuilding until the late 19th century.

6 West Bay to West Bexington

past Burton Bradstock and along Chesil Beach
5½ miles (8.75 km)

From West Bay, make for the high cliffs at the eastern end of the beach and follow the steep path to the cliff top.

On coming within sight of the caravan site go down to the beach and follow the fingerposts on the seaward side of the site, then along the river bank for about 200 yards (180 metres). Look out for a low stile on your right, which can sometimes be hidden by tents in summer. Go over this to cross the River Bridge, turning down the other side to rejoin the clifftop path and continue east.

You can also take a shortcut by following the river upstream (left), having crossed the footbridge, until you come into a walled lane at the end of the village of Burton Bradstock. You then turn seawards over a stile and up the hill beside a stone wall to come back to the top of Burton Cliff.

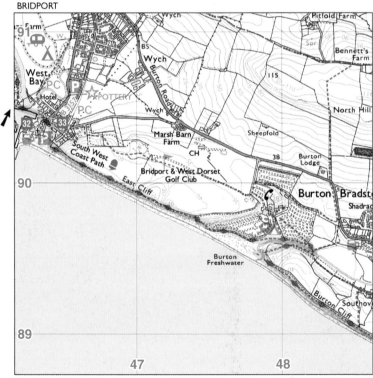

Contours are given in metres
The vertical interval is 5m

Burton Bradstock, with an attractive 1825 Wesleyan chapel, is an interesting village which played a major part in the cloth industry, and a spinning mill operated from 1794 until 1931. In addition, the first flax 'swingling' mill in the West Country was built here and opened in 1803. To swingle flax means to dress it, by a beating process which breaks down the non-fibrous parts of the stems of the flax. After this the flax stems are drawn through a kind of comb (a 'hackle') to give the long strands of fibre that make linen. The church **34** is also attractive, built mainly during the 14th and 15th centuries.

The cliff top on the western side of Burton Beach overhangs in places, and for safety the Coast Path has been taken back a little way from the cliff. Keep back from the cliff just before descending the rocky path which arrives at Burton Beach (NT).

On the eastern side of Burton Beach the path follows a stone wall and again keeps back from the cliff. Trampling feet on the immediate cliff top were causing serious erosion.

The path then leads into the Old Coastguard caravan site. Make your way across this, keeping close to the cliff until it drops down on to Cogden Beach (NT).

Contours are given in metres
The vertical interval is 5m

Cogden Beach is part of the famous natural pebble ridge called the Chesil Bank. Just after passing a track from the wood above, the Coast Path goes left and follows a fence to the landward side of the reed beds and Burton Mere. The route to West Bexington is along the back of the beach; previously it was difficult walking across the pebbles, but there is now a surfaced path along most of this section.

As you near West Bexington the fields may be flooded inland, and just before reaching the car park there is a large reed bed which is a nature reserve of the Dorset Wildlife Trust.

The great coastal monasteries

The path passes close to the ruins of parts of two very powerful medieval monasteries, at Abbotsbury, and further on at Little Bindon on the eastern side of Lulworth Cove (see page 76).

Abbotsbury

It is known that late Roman Britain was Christian, and it is possible that some of the Britons continued Christian traditions after the Roman withdrawal. It may be, therefore, that a church of St Peter was established during that time.

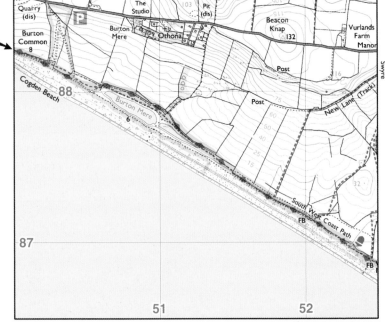

Contours are given in metres
The vertical interval is 5m

The Benedictine monastery was probably founded by monks from Cerne Abbas, just inland from Dorchester. We know there was a monastery here when William the Conqueror arrived, because Domesday gives us a detailed record of its wealth; there were eight manors, which included two mills, 15 hectares of meadow, much woodland and 'land to sixteen ploughs'.

In the following centuries the aristocracy and kings of England offered their protection and made substantial donations of land and money. The Benedictine monasteries were academic centres and manuscripts show that the monks of Abbotsbury reached great heights in art and learning.

Charters were granted giving many rights and privileges, and inside the parish church, which was separate from the abbey church, you will find a drawing showing how the abbey would have looked at its greatest.

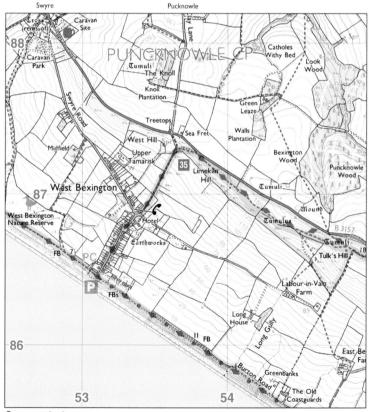

Contours are given in metres
The vertical interval is 5m

At this time there would have been people working wooden ploughs pulled by oxen on the hillsides above the village, where you can still see the terraced medieval fields.

During the 14th century there would also have been considerable building activity, with the sight of scaffolding around new stone buildings under construction. To the north of the abbey the village occupied approximately the same site as it does now, with its narrow streets leading to the market place, where you will now find the post office and The Ilchester Arms. A network of lanes would have radiated from the village to enable the abbot and his staff to go to supervise their farms, workshops and mills, and the lanes which lead off the main village street are the remnants of these ancient trackways.

In the 15th century the abbey appears to have gone through a period of great prosperity. It was then that the great Tithe Barn **53**, one of the largest in the country, was constructed, and this indicates that the agricultural production of the abbey and its associated establishments must have been considerable. St Catherine's Chapel **51**, on the hill above the village, was also built during this century and is worth a visit. It would appear, however, that in the late 1430s the abbot was letting the wealth of his domain lead to corrupt and dissolute habits. There were even hints that the abbot was not observing his vows of chastity.

At the beginning of the 16th century a gentleman called Thomas Strangways gave money for the establishment of a chantry so that the monks could pray for his soul daily, in perpetuity. Ironically, Henry VIII made Strangways' son Giles a commissioner for the Dissolution of the Dorset monasteries.

At the Dissolution the abbot became the vicar of the parish and Sir Giles Strangways was given a 20-year lease on the abbey with the condition that the buildings should be demolished. This he did, converting part into a large house for himself and retaining the half of the Tithe Barn which still stands. Much of the rest of the stonework of the abbey found its way into the houses in the village, as you will see when you walk along the village street.

The Abbey of Bindon

Cistercian monks arranged in 1149 to found a monastery at Lulworth Cove. The buildings on the eastern side of the Cove, at Little Bindon, which are immediately adjacent to the army range boundary, have been considered all that remains of the original foundation.

76

However, there is now some doubt about this. It is quite certain that an abbey was founded at Wool in 1172 and called Bindon. A charter of King John in 1216 set this out, and the buildings at Little Bindon, clearly medieval in origin, may have been established in association with the activities of the great abbey just inland. An aristocratic family called the de Newburghs, whose ancestors were personal friends of William the Conqueror, managed by the early 13th century to accumulate an estate which extended from Lulworth to Wool. In 1216 Robert de Newburgh granted land in three parishes to the abbey, and 17 years later made an additional grant of the eastern and southern parts of the parish of West Lulworth, including the land around Lulworth.

As the 13th century went on, his son Henry made further substantial donations of land, and towards the end of the century many other landowners did likewise. The abbey came to possess farms in many villages of Dorset and controlled several thousand acres of land, as well as some of the industrial sites of the time. Wareham fisheries are mentioned, and there is still a mill which belonged to them on the River Frome, beside the London–Weymouth railway.

They owned water meadows (some of which still exist in the Frome Valley), put much of the more fertile land under the plough and used the downland for sheep pasture.

In the late 13th and 14th centuries, however, numerous disputes arose over ownership, payment of dues and land boundaries, and on occasion the disputes became bitter.

In the 15th century things seemed to have settled down considerably as far as the conflict between the abbey and the landowners was concerned, and an orderly system of smallholding for tenantry appears to have developed, with a consequent rise in the fortunes of the abbey. The inventories prepared for the Dissolution by order of Henry VIII in 1539 showed that the abbots of Bindon were by then gaining a considerable income from leasing land for the grazing of sheep and other farming activities.

Two factors seem to have led to the demise of such abbeys. There was a threat from their power, which was often greater than that of the local landowners and aristocracy, and they were wealthy at a time when the king was short of cash. It would also seem that the religious intentions and piety of the monks and abbots was in doubt, and Henry VIII's argument with the Pope over his divorce was merely the last straw.

7 West Bexington to Portland Bill

past Abbotsbury and Langton Herring
20 ¹/₄ miles (32.6 km)

Between West Bexington and Osmington Mills you have the choice of two routes. One follows the coast closely, taking in Chesil Beach, the Fleet, the dramatic Isle of Portland and Weymouth. The second offers spectacular views of the coast from the ridge north of Weymouth, and passes by a remarkable

Chesil Beach (or Bank) with the Isle of Portland shimmering in the distance.

Contours are given in metres
The vertical interval is 5m

collection of archaeological monuments. Both routes have something to offer the Coast Path walker. Details of the coastal route are given first. The inland route, the South Dorset Ridgeway, is described in Chapter 9.

The Weymouth route of the Coast Path leaves West Bexington car park by following a track along the back of the Chesil Bank and continues behind the beach for some 2 miles (3 km). After Labour-in-Vain Farm, so called because the land needed much work for little return, the path passes the old coastguard houses and Lawrence's Cottage. Soon you come to more cottages and for about 600 yards the track becomes a surfaced road which soon branches northwards and inland.

This road leads to the Abbotsbury Sub-Tropical Gardens **50**, which are open every day except for a couple of weeks around Christmas/New Year and are well worth a visit. Refreshments are available inside.

The Coast Path continues along the beach for a further 200 yards and then branches inland, curving round to go almost due north-east. Above the path to the north-east is Chapel Hill with the 15th-century chapel of St Catherine **51** at its summit.

If you are anxious to make progress eastwards, follow the signs along the southern slopes of Chapel Hill, thus avoiding Abbotsbury. Having passed to the seaward side of Chapel Hill, the official route turns due north through the eastern edge of a small copse below the strip lynchets and behind the old mill. At the northern end of the miller's garden it crosses a small stream and turns south, crosses a stone stile and continues seawards to the Swannery car park.

A second permissive path diverges just north of the Chapel Withy Bed as a shortcut leading straight into the Swannery car park, near the medieval Abbot's Swannery **52**, which is also open to the public.

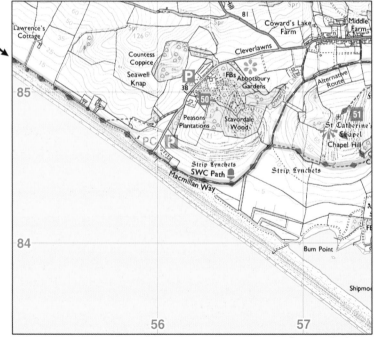

Contours are given in metres
The vertical interval is 5m

If, however, you wish to explore the ruins of the Abbey, see one of the largest tithe barns in England **53** and visit the rather beautiful village of Abbotsbury (see page 74), then detour north to the village.

Whichever way you have chosen to go through Abbotsbury, follow the signs away from the village to the Swannery car park, then follow the road a little way eastwards and leave it at Horsepool Farm buildings **54**. The route immediately strikes steeply up to the top of the ridge to the east. At the summit of the slope cross a stile and follow the upper side of a fence to the east.

Pass above Clayhanger Farm, behind which there are stiles to negotiate, and keep straight on along the ridge until a well-signed junction indicates where the path drops straight down the slope and to the eastern side of Hodder's Coppice.

At the southern edge of Hodder's Coppice the path crosses another stile to turn once again due east along the south of Ansty's Withy Bed, another small wood. Now cross a small

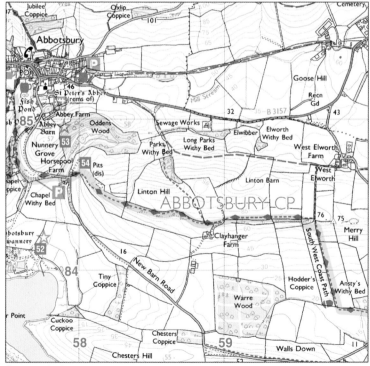

Contours are given in metres
The vertical interval is 5m

road at right angles and keep due east, staying parallel to the inland (northern) edge of Wyke Wood. Follow the edge of the wood, turning seawards round its eastern edge, and you will soon come into a valley which leads down to the Fleet lagoon.

You will see a group of buildings straight ahead. Make to the east of these buildings and follow the waymarks parallel to the stream, which is crossed by a small footbridge 300 yards back from the Fleet.

With the minor exceptions mentioned below, the route between this point, Langton Hive and Weymouth stays very close to the shoreline. At Langton Hive Point you will see a small landing stage below the former coastguard cottages and a bridleway which leads inland to Langton Herring and The Elm Tree pub.

The Coast Path continues close to the Fleet round a small cove, alongside a low stone wall and over a stile. After a short distance you come to Fleet House, now known after Falkner's novel *Moonfleet* as the Moonfleet Hotel, where refreshments may be obtained during opening hours **55**.

It is a half-hour walk along the Coast Path between the Moonfleet Hotel and the old Fleet Church at Butterstreet, where

Boats beside the Fleet.

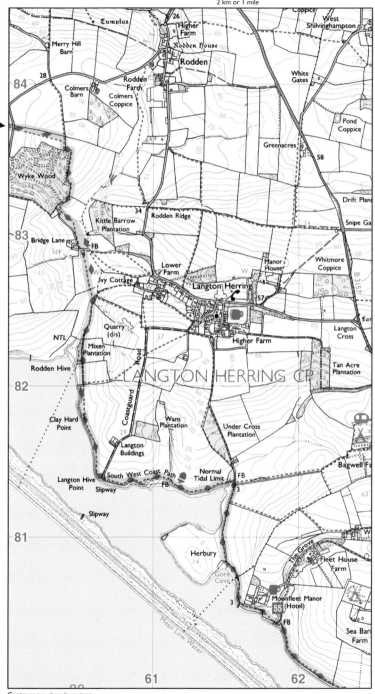

Contours are given in metres
The vertical interval is 5m

only the chancel remains after the rest of the church was destroyed by waves during a tempest in 1824 when the sea broke through the Chesil Bank. In the exciting Moonfleet story this is where the smugglers' kegs were hidden in the vaults.

The route crosses the small creek below the church, passes to the seaward side of a camping site at East Fleet Farm and close to a landing stage with a small group of fishermen's huts at Chickerell Hive Point. Just east of this and to the landward side of the path are the army huts of Chickerell Camp.

Shortly after this you will come to the Chickerell Rifle Range at Tidmoor Point **56**. If the red flags are flying, firing is taking place. A sentry should be posted on each side of the range and will direct you along the well waymarked Coast Path diversion.

If the red flags are not flying and no firing is taking place, the official route of the Coast Path keeps to the top of the low cliff around the firing range.

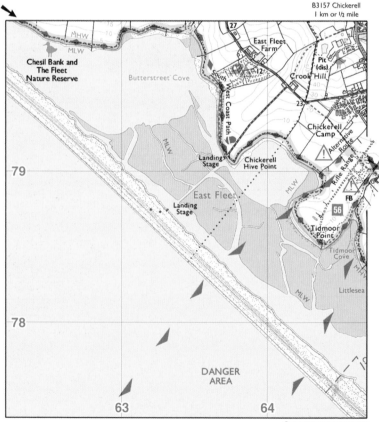

Contours are given in metres
The vertical interval is 5m

On the eastern side of the rifle range, cross a footbridge and a little further on enter the Littlesea Holiday Park, passing to the seaward side of the caravans and still keeping close to the Fleet. At the southern end of the campsite the Coast Path enters an attractive, overgrown area, emerging into open meadow.

Another military installation, the Royal Engineers Bridging Camp **57**, now has to be passed to the landward side. The Army has provided a fenced footpath all the way round the outside of the camp. This joins the access road to the camp at its entrance, and between the main entrance to the camp and the edge of the Fleet the Coast Path follows this road.

From the bridging camp to Ferry Bridge the path follows the Fleet through open fields bordered on the far side by the sub-urb of Wyke Regis, Weymouth, until it eventually reaches the Chesil Beach Holiday Centre. Keep to the seaward side of as many caravans as you can and follow the signs to the main

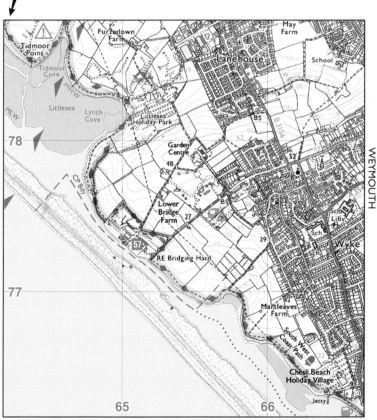

Contours are given in metres
The vertical interval is 5m

road. Now turn right towards Portland over the Ferry Bridge after passing the pub of that name.

The official route follows the combined cycleway and footpath immediately beside the busy main road. Once over the bridge, however, many walkers follow the shores of the harbour by walking along the old railway line, crossing back at the far end where this runs into an enclosed area.

You will see ships being repaired at the quays on the far side, prison ships, and many people wind-surfing with great skill.

Walking on the Chesil Bank itself can be very hard work .

Some 500–600 yards (450–550 metres) along the causeway to Portland is the Chesil Beach Centre, where displays explain the birds and the ecology of the Chesil Bank and the Fleet, an SSSI and European Marine Site. The car park here was originally cleared in early 1944 for marshalling American vehicles before, during and after the invasion of Normandy.

From the roundabout leading to the Sailing Academy a walk and cycleway leads along the edge of Portland Harbour and comes out at Henry VIII's Portland Castle. You will see ships being repaired on the quays on the far side, spare bits of the famous Mulberry Harbour and windsurfers.

Portland supplied the stone for thousands of famous buildings around the world, and particularly in London, where its white stone gave the Palace of Whitehall its name, as well as the road which leads to it. The Banqueting Hall in London, built to the designs of Inigo Jones in 1620, was one of the earlier Portland stone buildings to go up in the capital and a massive upsurge in demand for the Jurassic Portland stone occurred after the Great Fire of 1666, with Christopher Wren paying frequent visits to the island to select stone for his church building programme, including St Paul's Cathedral. He also became the Island's MP. The new London Bridge, the government buildings in New Delhi and the massive United Nations building in New York are some examples of the more famous structures using this stone. The bibliography at the end of this book lists a few of the books which detail the fascinating industrial archaeology and history of the island.

Having arrived at Chiswell, go right up Pebble Lane behind the Blue Fish Café and Restaurant past the fishermen's sheds to The Cove House Inn. Go up the steps beside the inn and turn left along the promenade. At the end of the promenade there is a gap in the sea defences where you can join a path which climbs up the hill closely following the garden boundaries of the

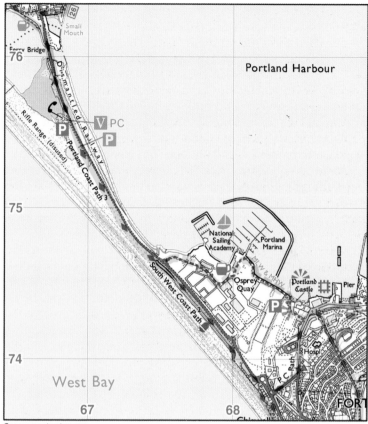

Contours are given in metres
The vertical interval is 5m

houses and a school, with wild land, screes of old quarries and the typical Portland huts to your right, used by fishermen and locals for their leisure time. When you get to the last houses go straight ahead and up some steps. At the top of these you come to a tarmac path where you turn right for Portland Bill. Follow the tarmac path up to the restored hand-crane which was used for loading stone on to horse-drawn trucks on the Merchant's railway which took the stone down to the harbour from here, one of many which you can trace on Portland. Here there is an arrow pointing to New Ground and East Cliff.

I am going to suggest that you go around Portland clockwise, so that you can get a look at the superb scenery of Purbeck, have the coast on your left for a change, and get a good idea of the geography of the next part of your walk eastwards. Then, before tackling the next challenge, you will have one last chance to admire the scenery of the Chesil and Fleet, and perhaps the whole of Lyme Bay, before finally going east. So go down the main road for 20 or 30 yards (15–25 metres). Cross the road and go up the stony path opposite. Look back to see a fine view of the Fleet lagoon and Chesil Beach stretching back to Bridport Harbour and, on a clear day, the whole of Lyme Bay from Start Point or Berry Head. Closer to hand is the sculpture, *The Spirit of Portland*, with the working stonemasons.

At the top of the stony path you come to a narrow tarmac road. Go right up this road and then left along the grassy banks in front of the Portland Heights Hotel, going parallel to Yeates Road and towards an obelisk commemorating Portlanders who died in the wars of the 20th century. From this point you can see the man-made causeway which brought you to Portland. Before a bridge was built to connect Portland with England in 1839 you came by ferry. Next a railway was built as far as the bottom of the hill, extended to the top of the Island early in the 20th century. Now follow the road briefly and then the road-side path past the New Ground viewing point and car parks. Keep straight on along the tarmac road eastwards past all the car parks on your left and over two stone railway bridges.

When you come to the car park at the rear entrance to the Verne Prison, turn sharp right along the road and you will see the original Portland Prison, which is now a Young Offenders' Institute (YOI). You can identify the building by the tall chimney-like structures, which in fact are ventilators for the Victorian cells.

The Verne Prison, which is now behind you, was an army barracks constructed, like hundreds of south coast military structures, during the nineteenth century to counter a per-ceived threat from France. It had all the latest in defensive structures and devices of the time. You can find out more about this era by visiting the Nothe Fort by Weymouth Harbour. The fortifications were never really used for their original purpose, but served as a depot until just after the Second World War, when it was vacated by the Army and became a prison, almost completely hidden in a quarried hollow in the hill top. Inside some of the original buildings have found uses as classrooms and prison accommodation, combined with newer purpose-built blocks of bed-sits and training workshops.

Keep going straight towards the YOI. On your right you may see an active quarry. Keep on along the quarry track and turn left past some massive stone blocks towards the old engine winding house. This housed the power units which used to move the

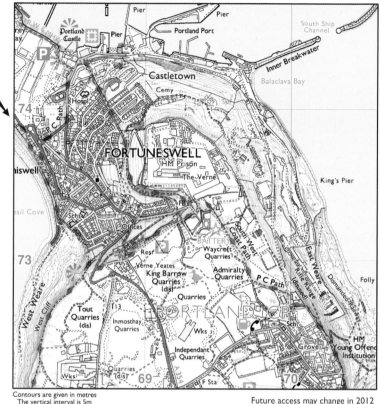

Contours are given in metres
The vertical interval is 5m

Future access may change in 2012

stone trucks by cable up and down the inclined track below. Behind the engine house go through a gap in the high stone wall and left again to follow the seaward YOI boundary fence. Below you are the Weirs (coastal screes and slopes), where quarrymen exploited the Portland stone and loaded it on to barges from small quays with the typical hand-cranes, one of which can still be seen below. Looking east there are superb views of the chalk and limestone cliffs of Purbeck as far as St Aldhelm's Head.

The first high chalk cliffs you can see are at Ringstead (White Nothe) and the high ridge further back is near Tyneham, with Kimmeridge Bay identifiable by its clifftop tower on a clear day.

Continue past the YOI on a tarmac road and then a narrow clifftop path which broadens out. You may see the Channel Island ferries and small fishing and sailing boats on their way to and from Weymouth and Portland harbours. Below is the track bed of the railway built early in the 20th century to link the top of the island into the national rail network. As you come to the top of the slopes ahead you will see Portland Lighthouse with its distinctive red stripe. Where a steep track joins the clifftop path, take the narrow stony path which forks left immediately south of the track to take you to Church Ope Cove. Ope derives from opening, as in gap in the cliff. The path joins the railway track briefly and you should make for the ivy-covered ruins of the 15th-century Rufus or Bow and Arrow Castle, built by Richard, Duke of York, as a coastal defence against French raids near the end of the Hundred Years' War. There's not much of the castle left, but look out for the gun loops, the small round holes from which small arms could be fired.

Branch left to go to the seaward side of the castle remains. The official route goes down the steep concrete steps to the cove and then along the undercliff, rising to join the road above, which it follows for a short distance.

You may like first to make a detour up under the archway to see the tiny thatched Portland Museum, famous as the setting of the home of the heroines in Thomas Hardy's *The Well-Beloved,* and a fascinating display of Portland's long and varied history. The museum was a gift from Marie Stopes, who lived in the Old Higher Lighthouse at Portland Bill. Also worth viewing from the road just south is Pennsylvania Castle, designed by James Wyatt in 1800 for the Governor of the island, John Penn, grandson of the founder of Pennsylvania. Just south of Pennsylvania Castle you will see on the left of the road the remains of the old 'bankers' – platforms used to load the horse-driven carts with stone.

Having got this far, you may decide to follow the road towards Portland Bill for a short distance, although Church Ope Cove has more historic secrets to reveal if you have time to explore there as well.

Either way, follow the road towards Portland Bill until you see a clifftop house standing on its own. Just beyond this the Coast Path follows the rough track leading seawards. Just follow this through all the old quarries and then along the cliff top, past the stone crane which is now used to lower boats into the water, until you get to Portland Bill. The three lighthouses are all attractive, as is the Pulpit Rock just beyond the 135-foot 1905 lighthouse. The upper and lower lights were built first, in 1716, and coal-fired, then rebuilt in 1869. Portland is famous as a migration site for birds, with many rare sightings, and the lower lighthouse is now an observatory. The lights were built to work together and were replaced by the currently working one, which is sometimes open to the public and well worth a visit.

Tar Rocks

Clay Ope

Quarries

Wks

Grove

Independant
Quarries

F Sta

Quarries
(dis)

Wks

Bowers
Quarries

Cemy

Coll

Broadcroft Quarry
Butterfly Reserve

Yeolands
Quarry

Easton

Blacknor

Silklake Quarries

Sch

PO

Bottom
Coombe
Quarries

Mutton Cove

Lawnsheds

Perryfield
Quarries

Rufus Castle
(rems of)
Church
(rems of)

Weston

67

Quarry
(dis)

Church Ope
Cove

Suckthumb
Quarry
(dis)

69

Lawnsheds

Southwell

Coombefield Quarries
(Stone)

S W C Path

Southwell Landslip

P C Path

Quarries
(dis)

Sch

Freshwater Bay

0

Sweet Hill

Quarries
(dis)

God Nore

Portland Coast Path

59

S W C Path

Limekiln Cave

Field System

Sand Holes

lsend Cove

Lawnsheds

54

Culver Well

28

Quarries
(dis)

out
on

Lloyds
Cottage

Lawnsheds

Cave Hole

9

Rocket Post

Bird
Observatory

ock

Land Mark

ortland Bill

68

69

70

tours are given in metres
e vertical interval is 5m

91

The magnificent western cliffs of Portland.

8 Portland Bill to Osmington Mills

Route improvements planned for 2012. Follow any new signs
15¾ miles (25.3 km)

From Portland Bill make for the clifftop Coastwatch lookout on the horizon behind The Pulpit Inn and then go to the seaward side of the Upper Lighthouse. Follow the wide grassy track with magnificent views of Lyme Bay and just keep to the cliff top all the way to Chesil Cove. The path goes quite goes quite close to the cliff through the quarries and under one of the massive stone arches. If you are planning to visit Portland Castle or stay at the youth hostel or accommodation in Castletown, you can retrace your steps to the back door of the Verne Prison and follow the path round the western side of the Verne ramparts down the old railway incline into Castletown.

Castletown has several pubs and shops and a summer ferry service to Weymouth harbour. There is also a path along the shores of Portland Harbour, which links through to the Coast

Contours are given in metres
The vertical interval is 5m

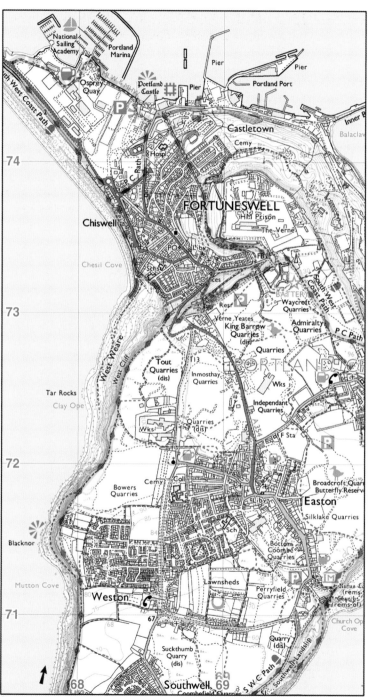

Contours are given in metres
The vertical interval is 5m

95

Path by the roundabout on the causeway in due course. Birdwatchers use this to view wintering wildfowl on the harbour's waters. Henry VIII's Portland Castle, tiny and unassuming from the outside, has a fascinating past stretching from 1540 to the 1940s. This is excellently explained by audio guide and first-class displays inside this ancient stronghold. You can also get good views of Portland Harbour from the ramparts.

Otherwise cross the causeway and Ferry Bridge again (see map on page 87). Going east from Ferry Bridge to Weymouth harbour is an easy walk of some 2 miles (3 km). At Ferry Bridge follow the waterside path east and the shores of Portland Harbour by the sea, partly using a disused railway line. Continue to Old Castle Road, which leads to Sandsfoot Castle **58**. Henry VIII's Sandsfoot Castle was built in 1539, when an invasion was feared, and it is said that fragments of medieval stonework in its walls were brought from Bindon Abbey at Wool.

Follow Old Castle Road for a short distance more, and then continue along the path and roads which follow the shores of Portland Harbour between Sandsfoot and the Nothe Gardens. At the far end of these is the Nothe Fort **59**, built to counter the Napoleonic threat and now open to the public, with displays on its role in maritime defence. The nearby ferry crosses the harbour for a small fee. Weymouth harbour is quite attractive – fishing boats are often tied up to the quay beside the ferries. There are several harbourside pubs and a museum devoted to shipwrecks and diving, which is worth a visit.

It was George Ill who started the fashion for Weymouth as a seaside resort. He came year after year. The town was so grateful that a statue to him was erected at the western end of the sea front. If you look to the east you may be able to see the chalk figure of George III on horseback cut in the hillside.

Make now for the Esplanade of Weymouth, one of the finest 18th-century seaside façades of any resort in England, although in the summer it can be rather noisy and crowded.

If you are starting or finishing your journey at this point, there are hourly trains from Weymouth to London (three hours) and a two-hourly service to Bristol, Cardiff and points beyond via Yeovil, sometimes in trains decorated externally with scenes from the South West Coast Path. In addition there are daily fast direct services by train to all parts of the country via Poole. There are also daily connections to all areas of the country by coach, and ferry services to the Channel Islands.

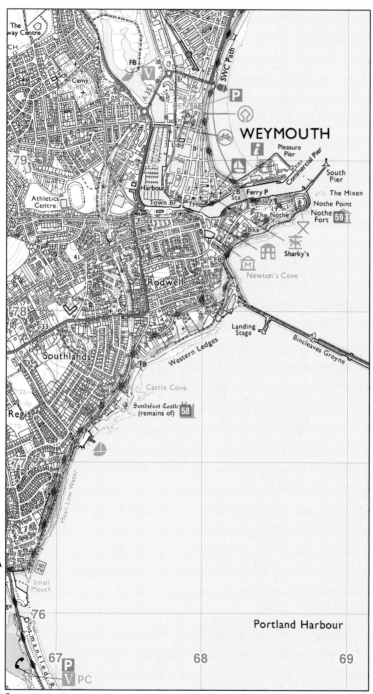

WEYMOUTH

Pleasure Pier

Commercial Pier

South Pier

The Mixen

Nothe Point

Nothe Fort **59**

The Nothe

Sharky's

Newton's Cove

Ferry P

Sta

Bks

Harbour

Town Br

TH

Athletics Centre

ARTS CENTRE

Liby

SWC Path

79

CH.

Sch

Cemy

The ...way Centre

FB

V

P

Rodwell

Sch

78

Southlands

FB

Western Ledges

Landing Stage

Bincleaves Groyne

Castle Cove

Sandsfoot Castle (remains of) **58**

Regis

Mean Low Water

26

Small Mouth

...ge

76

Dismantled R...

67

P

V PC

68

69

Portland Harbour

Contours are given in metres
The vertical interval is 5m

To continue east from Weymouth follow the sea wall in front of Lodmoor. The lagoons on the landward side are the site of an RSPB reserve. At the eastern end of the sea wall, the path follows the road and grassy areas beside it heading east, and there are signs to the remains of the Roman temple of Jordan Hill. Follow the sea wall to Overcombe Corner and then onwards to Bowleaze Cove.

The path then goes up a road parallel to the coast in the fields inland and north of the Riviera Hotel. The cliffs have been eroding with spectacular speed for the next 2 miles (3 km) to Osmington Mills and a route has been signed at the top of the fields. At the outdoor education centre **60** the path remains near the cliff, but after that you have to go to the top of the fields again.

Two-thirds of a mile (1 km) east of the centre, and after passing Black Head, look out for a stile across a fence on the landward side of the clifftop field above Osmington Mills (see map on page 115). Follow a narrow path down to the road. Keep right where the path rejoins the eastern end of the inland route, and turn right down the road to The Smugglers Inn.

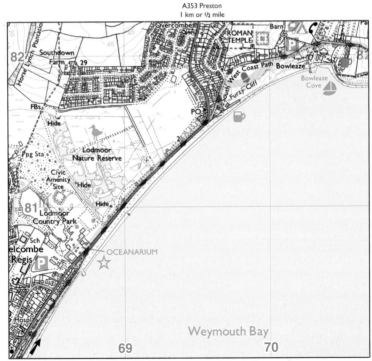

Contours are given in metres
The vertical interval is 5m

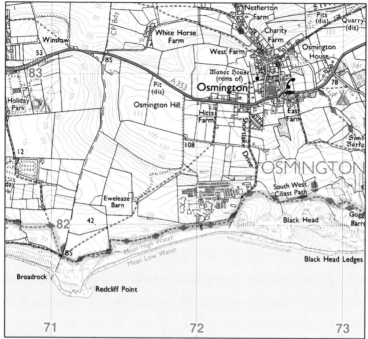

Contours are given in metres
The vertical interval is 5m

The ports of Weymouth Bay

Many of the towns and villages through which the Coast Path passes were important ports before the coming of the railways. It is only during this century that their significance has dwindled, with tourism taking the first place in their economies, although Weymouth and Poole still have ferry services to France and the Channel Islands, as well as freight cargo shipments.

In Roman times Kimmeridge was an industrial centre. No evidence of a Roman quay remains, but various unsuccessful attempts were made through the ages to develop it as a commercial port and traces of the quays can still be found there. A safer haven and natural miniature harbour was at Lulworth Cove, still used for this purpose today.

Portland Harbour was built by convicts between 1849 and the harbour at Weymouth must have been used in Roman times since a Roman road, still used, leads from Dorchester, which had straight and direct road links with London.

The port first made news when a ship unloading here brought the Black Death to England in 1348. In medieval times Weymouth

Weymouth is still a bustling port, where the local fishing industry thrives and the har

on the western side of the River Wey and Melcombe Regis on the eastern were both important ports. There seems to have been some decline in the late medieval period, but both harbours were active again during Elizabethan and Jacobean times.

We must remember that until the coming of the train and efficient road services, one of the best ways of getting to other parts of the country, including London, would have been by boat. The young architect and author Thomas Hardy travelled in this way from London to Dorchester.

Weymouth was also important in maintaining British contacts with the Channel Islands, particularly during times of tension with France, and when we were being friendly towards our neighbours there would have been a lot of trade with Normandy.

The port of Weymouth was in decline when quite suddenly doctors produced a theory that resting by the sea and sea

busy with pleasure boats and cross-Channel ferries.

bathing were good for you, and thus Melcombe Regis became a fashionable resort. When the railway arrived in 1857, providing a direct link to London via Dorchester and Westbury, as well as links to many other parts of the south coast of England via Southampton, the tourist trade was given an enormous boost.

The line that brought Brunel's Great Western Railway to Weymouth from thriving 19th-century Bristol and fashionable Bath Spa is still in operation and it is an attractive journey, as it meanders through rural Dorset, Somerset and Wiltshire. It was in order to boost trade on this line that the Great Western initiated their own Weymouth to Cherbourg service and 11 years later, in 1889, started their London–Weymouth–Channel Islands run, the fastest land-sea route.

The port of Weymouth is also still a haven for fishing boats as well as pleasure boats of all sizes, and it continues to thrive.

9 West Bexington to Osmington Mills via the Ridgeway (inland route)

past Abbotsbury Castle and Upwey
17 miles (27.3 km)

If you have chosen to take the inland route from West Bexington rather than the coastal route via Chesil and Portland described in the last two chapters, then you will be following the South Dorset Ridgeway, which offers an attractive alternative, rejoining the coastal route at Osmington Mills.

Rather than the flat, relatively easy walking of the coastal route, the Dorset Ridgeway runs, for the most part, over open downland and involves some quite steep climbs and descents. As compensation, it offers, on clear days, superb views of the sea and the Isle of Portland, as well as distant views of the hills of inland Dorset. It also takes you past one of the most remarkable conglomerations of archaeological monuments in the whole of Britain. Even those who are not particularly interested in such things are likely to be impressed by views of Maiden Castle, one of the largest and most distinctive hill forts in Britain, as well as by the many other intriguing remains to be found along the route.

To follow the South Dorset Ridgeway (inland route) of the Coast Path, go up the road above the beach car park at West Bexington. Where the road turns left, keep straight on up a track, forking right just before the top. A gateway on your right leads to the level meadow land of Limekiln Hill. This is National Trust land and they have restored the lime kiln with the help of the British Trust for Conservation Volunteers. You will find it just over the edge of the slope on the seaward side of the path **35**.

These lime kilns were once extensively used to produce lime for whitewash, plaster and mortar, or for reducing the acidity of some soils to improve cropping. Fuel and limestone would be unloaded from horse carts at the top end and the finished product would be extracted from the bottom. The coal used in this area was 'culm', a low-grade anthracite from Pembrokeshire. It was brought in by schooner, until rail transport arrived in the 19th century. During the 20th century the production of lime became concentrated on large centres, and cement produced in a few works replaced the use of lime in building.

Now keep to the seaward edge of the meadow, cross the stone stile and keep straight on along the ridge towards a group of tumuli on the hill top. From here the path follows the

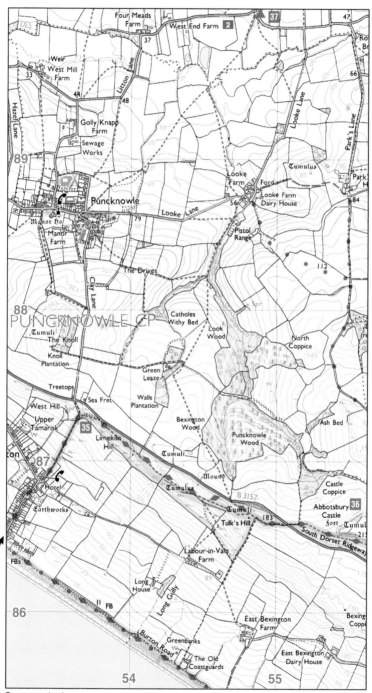

Contours are given in metres
The vertical interval is 5m

103

landward side of a substantial drystone wall until it crosses the Abbotsbury–Bridport road by a stile on the southern side of the road and a bridlegate on the northern side.

You now follow the southern ramparts of the Iron Age hill fort called Abbotsbury Castle **36**, and go straight across a small lane.

You can read more about these hill forts on page 120. This particular fort was never finished and its builders seem to have been in an enormous hurry. If you look carefully you will see that loads of soil were evidently dumped on the banks, but never levelled or finished in the normal way. Did the enemy arrive too soon? Was all this happening the day the Britons were losing against the Romans at Maiden Castle?

The lane mentioned above is an 'Unclassified County Road' and is a delightful green lane for much of the 3 miles (5 km) north to Litton Cheney Youth Hostel **37** (see top of map on page 103). Allow 50 minutes for the journey to the hostel, heading north, through Park's Dairy Farm, until you reach a T-junction. Turn left and the hostel is about 500 yards away, on the corner opposite the village pub and a small stream.

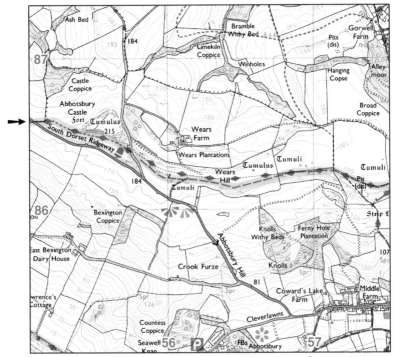

Contours are given in metres
The vertical interval is 5m

The Coast Path itself keeps to the top of the ridge of Wears Hill. At White Hill the ridge broadens. Keep just to the seaward side of the crest of the ridge across a very large field to a corner where the bridleway from Abbotsbury joins the path. Fork left along the fence to the Bishop's Road. Go ahead for 40 yards (35 metres) and turn right through a bridlegate and stay just below a fence at the head of a terraced valley. At the top left-hand corner of this wild area the Coast Path crosses a stile and joins a gated farm track. Halfway along is a prehistoric stone circle. Continue straight on to the southern side of a group of farm buildings.

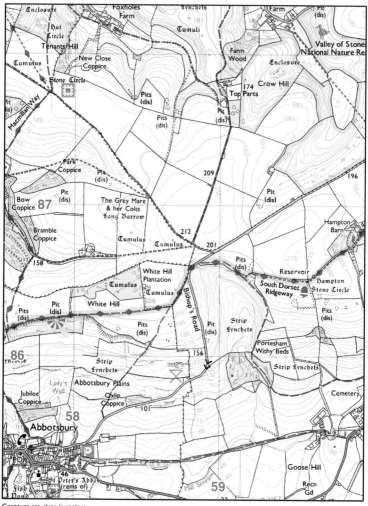

Contours are given in metres
The vertical interval is 5m

Cross another road by going a few yards to the north and then strike due east again towards the Hardy Monument **39**.

The path crosses one field at Portesham Hill and comes to some stone stiles. The Coast Path leads due east for the length of a wall until it comes to Black Down Barn, where it branches north-east through a plantation to the Hardy Monument.

First you may wish to visit the Hell Stone **38**, a reconstructed burial chamber. There is a permissive path which leads diagonally across the field to the south-east from the stone stile. The Hell Stone is a substantial cromlech and, although it was reconstructed in the 19th century, there are indications that the present structure strongly resembles the original, which would have been covered by a long mound of earth. (Read more about this on page 112.)

From the Hell Stone continue due north along the wall next to which it stands, and another stone stile brings you back out on the Coast Path, where you turn due east.

The monument **39** is to Admiral Thomas Hardy, of Nelson's flagship at Trafalgar. Hardy was born nearby at Kingston Russell

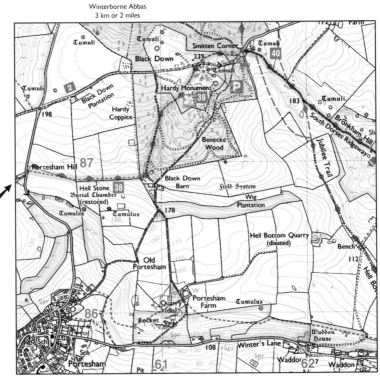

Contours are given in metres
The vertical interval is 5m

House in 1760 and left to go to sea at the age of 12, although he came back to school at the age of 13 for another three years. He then took to sea again and in due course joined the Royal Navy, becoming a lieutenant at the age of 21. Two years later he met Nelson and the two worked together until the Battle of Trafalgar in 1805. Hardy subsequently retired to Portesham, just below this monument, and died in 1839 at the age of 79.

The official Coast Path crosses the road opposite the Hardy Monument for a short way to return at Smitten Corner, whence it travels south-eastwards down a track beside a group of very distinctive tumuli **40**.

The track stays on the ridge for 3 miles (5 km), and remains a bridleway throughout that length. It passes many more tumuli

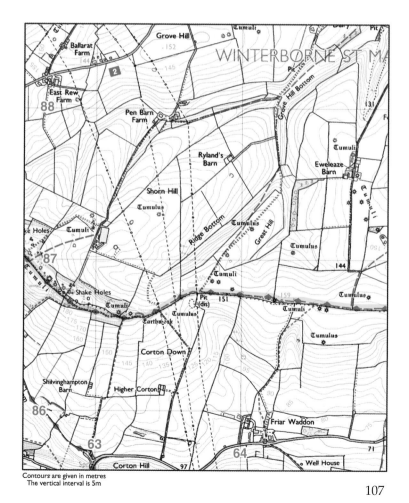

Contours are given in metres
The vertical interval is 5m

and from the bridleway it is possible to make easy diversions to Martinstown (which has a medieval church), Maiden Castle hill fort **41** and Dorchester.

After 2¹/₂ miles (4 km) along Ridge Hill, the path crosses the B3159 Upwey-Martinstown road beside a Weymouth Borough Council marker **42**. The route goes straight through the gate opposite and continues along the ridge until it meets a stony track at right angles. This track is the original route of the old Roman road that was constructed to connect Dorchester to the port of Weymouth **43**.

The Coast Path now crosses the busy A354 Dorchester–Weymouth road over a bridge. More or less straight ahead is the old road, which the official route rejoins about ³/₄ mile (1 km) west of the bridge. To stick to the official route, turn south down the bridleway towards Weymouth for about 400 yards and then turn left (west) through the fields.

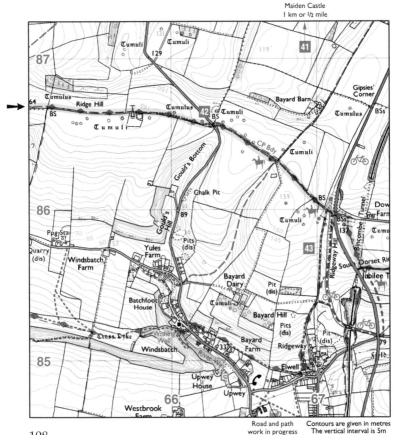

Maiden Castle
1 km or 1/2 mile

Road and path
work in progress

Contours are given in metres
The vertical interval is 5m

Rejoin the ridge-top road for a short distance beside the golf course until you reach the next junction. Turn due south down the bridleway opposite the road from Dorchester and follow it down into the village of Bincombe, where you will see the church **44** ahead. Pass to the north of the church and keep on up the farm track. This is clearly waymarked through a number of fields, giving good views of strip lynchets, the field systems of medieval farming **45**.

Carry straight on until you come to the top of a steep slope. The official route of the path bears north-east to Greenhill Barton, a group of isolated barns, but an alternative route drops straight down and proceeds round the seaward side of a small knoll to rejoin the bridleway along West Hill. To the south of this is the hill fort of Chalbury **46**.

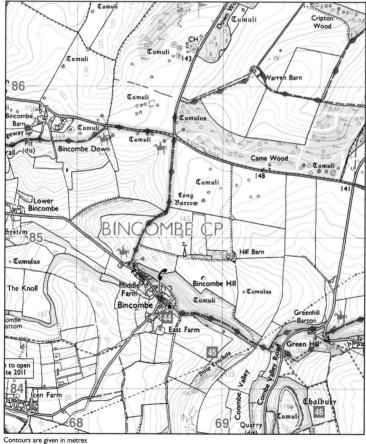

Contours are given in metres
The vertical interval is 5m

109

The path follows the bridleway for a further 1¼ miles (2 km), keeping more or less to the top of the steep slope of the ridge overlooking Sutton Poyntz. You pass a number of tumuli **47** to the landward side of the path and reach Northdown Barn, which is ruined, then follow the chalk tracks which lead eastwards to White Horse Hill. The Coast Path passes along the northern edge of a large field which stands on top of the hill immediately above the White Horse **48**.

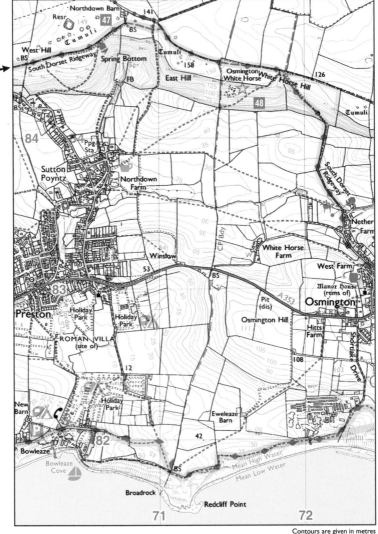

Contours are given in metres
The vertical interval is 5m

The White Horse, cut in the turf on the hills behind Osmington, has George III riding it and was dug in the hillside to commemorate his many visits at the end of the 18th century.

At the eastern end of this large field there is a gateway which comes out to a junction of four bridleways. The Coast Path takes the bridleway leading down the steeper slope to the south-east, which is a rugged farm track leading down between hedges to the village of Osmington.

Find your way to the south-east corner of Osmington, opposite The Sunray Inn. Then walk about 120 yards eastwards along the main road. About 25 yards past the entrance to Craigs Farm Dairy is a footbridge which gives access to the path, which then follows a hedgerow all the way to the settlement of Osmington Mills. Walk down the road to The Smuggler's Inn **49** and you are back on the coastal route of the Coast Path.

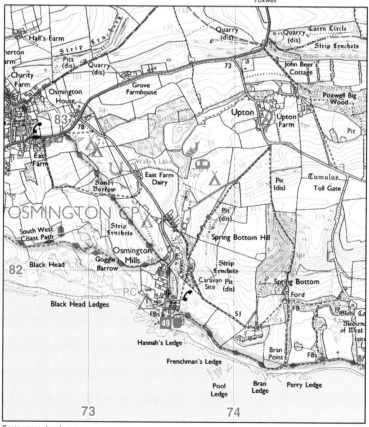

Contours are given in metres
The vertical interval is 5m

Ancient rites on the Dorset and East Devon coasts

At nearly every point on this Coast Path you will be within sight of some evidence of prehistoric occupation.

The long barrows

Some of the most ancient and rare prehistoric remains you will see are the long barrows. These are the burial mounds of the New Stone Age (Neolithic period), which lasted from 5000 to 2200 BC in Britain.

Excavations have revealed collections of bones and it seems likely that the practice of allowing the bones first to be pecked clean of flesh after death, as still happens in some Far Eastern countries today, was common in Stone Age times. Subsequently they were buried and covered by the mound.

In some cases the mounds had internal chambers. The Hell Stone **38** on Portesham Hill, just west of the Hardy Monument, is a 19th-century reconstruction made from the stone of the structure found in position on the site. Note the round barrows dating from the later Bronze Age grouped around the Hell Stone.

There is another long barrow, not far from the path, on the ridge to the west of the White Horse.

The round barrows

Round barrows were constructed later, in the Bronze Age (2200–650 BC), but it is clear they were deliberately placed near the long barrows. The concentration of round barrows along and near the South Dorset Ridgeway is clearly visible from a great distance. During very clear weather the views from the site are still spectacular, and then you can understand why prehistoric people considered this hill top to be of particular significance in their spiritual lives.

By comparing these with similar monuments in other parts of the country, such as Wales and Cornwall, and in Brittany, we can deduce that they were normally used for the burial of extremely important people. Clearly, if just anybody had the right to be buried in this way there would be far more mounds and larger numbers of interments would be found in them.

If you look at them carefully you will see a variety of different forms. A 'bowl' barrow is simply a circular mound; a 'bell' barrow has, or once had, a ditch around it; a 'disk' barrow has a much lower mound and a ditch, which in turn is surrounded by

The Hell Stone burial chamber, a 19th-century reconstruction of a prehistoric barrow.

a bank; and the last type is called the 'pond' barrow and is just a hollow surrounded by a bank. Sometimes subsequent ploughing has altered the appearance, but careful archaeological excavation often reveals the original forms.

Along the South Dorset Ridgeway you will see one of the greatest concentrations of round barrows in the British Isles, with nearly 200 on the Ridgeway itself and a further 200 within a very short distance. Allowing for destruction over the ages, both natural and man-induced, there may originally have been more than 1,000 of them. Clearly, 4,000 years ago this part of England had a very special importance for the inhabitants of quite a large area.

Virtually all the mounds that you will see as you follow the Coast Path from Exmouth to Studland can be assumed to be evidence of a Bronze Age civilisation whose lifestyle can be reconstructed by careful observation of the objects which have been found in them during archaeological excavations. In the text I have referred to them loosely as 'tumuli'.

10 Osmington Mills to Lulworth Cove

past White Nothe and Durdle Door
6 miles (9.6 km)

The car park at Osmington Mills belongs to The Smugglers Inn and is primarily for the use of customers during opening hours, although the publican has no objection to customers going for a walk between times. You will also find toilets, a shop and a campsite in the village.

Going east, proceed nearly to the front door of the pub and then skirt round the landward side of the bars, by the old wooden coastguard cottages. The Coast Path goes to the top, seaward side of the first field and then keeps to the cliff top for a further 1¼ miles (2 km).

Just to the east of the modern settlement of Ringstead **61** there is a field beside the Coast Path, enclosed on all sides by woods. This is the site of the deserted medieval village of Ringstead.

Osmington and Ringstead from White Nothe.

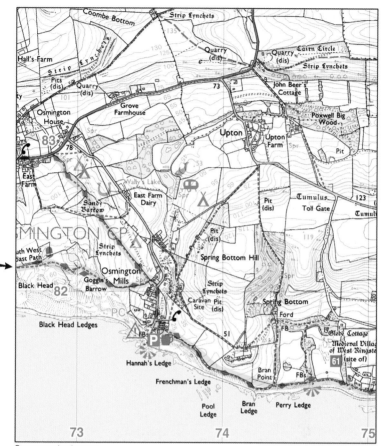

Contours are given in metres
The vertical interval is 5m

Local legend has it that French pirates burnt the village to the ground, killed all the men and carried off the women and children.

It is, however, more likely that such villages were deserted partly because of the Black Death, or, even more mundanely and commonly, because of economic and agricultural changes that destroyed the livelihood of the inhabitants. Records for Ringstead, however, show that the actual population change of the area was minimal, and so the desertion of the village may be better explained by the dispersion of the population as they went to live in places more convenient to their work, scattered around the immediate locality. When the grass is short and the weather dry, the traces of the village street and the cottages can still be seen.

At the new settlement of Ringstead, the Coast Path goes inland for a little way and then strikes eastwards along a track to the seaward side of the car park. The track passes a small caravan site and goes through an area of thicket.

The Coast Path emerges after the thicket on to a lawn beside Burning Cliff, so called because it ignited spontaneously in the 19th century and became a popular tourist attraction. The undercliff here is National Trust land and a narrow path gives access to the beach at this point **62**.

Meanwhile the Coast Path follows a track east, to the landward side of the chapel of St Catherine, and keeps straight on where the track bears inland, beside a bungalow, before emerging at the gates of Holworth House.

Between this point and Durdle Door it is 3 miles (5 km) and the route stays on the cliff top throughout.

From the former coastguard cottages at White Nothe **63** there are superb views of the nature reserve, and a precipitous path

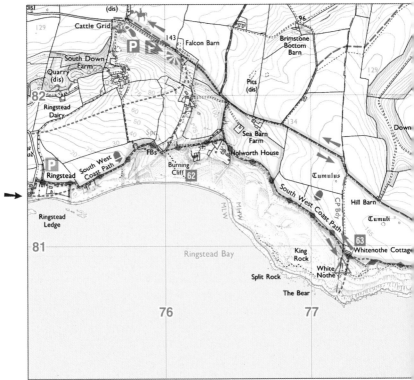

Contours are given in r
The vertical interval is

leads westwards under King Rock and back down to the beach. It is easier and safer, however, to find your way from the bottom rather than the top, and if you have descended to the beach at the western end you may like to rejoin the Coast Path by this route. It is, however, a climb that should be avoided by those who suffer from vertigo.

From White Nothe the Coast Path keeps to the cliff edge except to skirt around the back of West Bottom. There will be no problems in either direction, and this is one of the quieter parts of the Coast Path.

Looking south you see the Isle of Portland across Weymouth Bay.

Looking east the first distinctive feature is Bat's Head: a triangular cliff jutting out of the sea with a narrow cave going through it. Beyond that is Durdle Door and the high ground of Hambury Tout, followed by the Lulworth Army Ranges. This spot has great wild flowers, wild roe deer and rare chalk downland butterflies and moths. There are grassy hollows where you can picnic while enjoying the stunning new views.

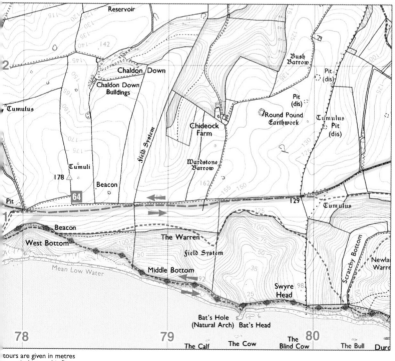

tours are given in metres
e vertical interval is 5m

The path drops steeply into a small valley called Scratchy Bottom, just west of Durdle Door, a limestone archway pierced over the years by the waves to make it one of the most famous landmarks on the south coast of England. The name 'Durdle' comes from the Saxon *durch* meaning 'through' and 'Door' is the more modern equivalent to signify the opening in the rock.

There is a track leading up to the nearby car park and caravan site, where there are toilets, telephones and refreshments. Meanwhile, heading east, the Coast Path stays on top of the cliff, rising to Hambury Tout. Below there are dramatic chalk cliffs of many colours, with Durdle Door in the near distance, Bat's Head with its small cave in the middle distance and White Nothe, Weymouth Bay and Portland completing the scene.

At this point Lulworth Cove and the Army Ranges come into sight. At the far side of the Cove car park is the barn-like Lulworth Heritage Centre. This has excellent displays, with first-class illustrations, on the history and geology of Lulworth. It explains and brings to life the rock formations, the pre-history, family history and natural history of the Lulworth Estate and is without a doubt the best centre on the Jurassic Coast. It is open almost throughout the year. See www.lulworth.co.uk

At Lulworth Cove it is worth exploring Stair Hole with its caves pierced through the limestone mass, allowing the sea to wash out the softer clays behind. This may be what Lulworth Cove looked like millions of years ago, before the sea penetrated as far as the chalk cliffs of Bindon Hill behind. From Stair Hole one has a superb view of the Lulworth Crumple, which illustrates the geological folding that gives this area such an unusual and varied landscape. Lulworth Cove itself has full facilities, including refreshments.

Just inland at East Lulworth is the 17th-century ruin of Lulworth Castle. In the grounds is a church with a 15th-century tower and font, although the remainder was restored in the last century. The family who owned the castle were friendly with George III and are one of the great old Catholic families of England. It is said that George III gave permission for the construction of a Catholic church in the grounds of the castle so long as it did not have the appearance of being a church.

The poet John Keats spent his last days in England at Lulworth, having come ashore while becalmed on his way to Italy, where it was thought his illness might be cured.

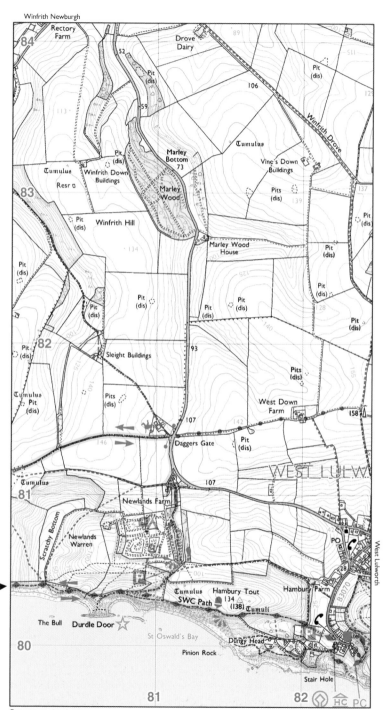

Winfrith Newburgh

Rectory Farm
84

Drove Dairy
89

Pit (dis)
115

52

106

125

59

Marley Bottom 73

Tumulus

Vine's Down Buildings

Winfrith Drove

Tumulus
Winfrith Down Buildings

Resr

Marley Wood

137

Pits (dis)
139

Pit (dis)

83

Winfrith Hill
Pit (dis)

Marley Wood House

Pit (dis)

134

125

Pit (dis)

128

Pit (dis)

Pit (dis)

Pit (dis)

Pit (dis)

Pit (dis)

140

Pit (dis)

82
Pit (dis)

Sleight Buildings

93

156

Pits (dis)

West Down Farm

158

Tumulus
Pit (dis)

Pits (dis)

146

107

Daggers Gate

Pit (dis)

142

WEST LULW

Tumulus

107

81

Newlands Farm

Scratchy Bottom

Newlands Warren

PO

West Lulworth

P

100

Tumulus
Hambury Tout

Hambury Farm

SWC Path
134
(138) Tumuli

28

B3070

The Bull
Durdle Door

Tel

80
St Oswald's Bay

Dungy Head

Pinion Rock

Stair Hole

81
82
HC PC

Contours are given in metres
The vertical interval is 5m

119

Pre-Roman times on the coast

On virtually every day while walking along this Coast Path you will see at least one prehistoric hill fort. These vary from quite simple enclosures with one bank and ditch around them, as at Branscombe, to the large, impressive establishments with many ditches, as at Maiden Castle, which is Iron Age in origin.

Signs of occupation have been found in a number of the hill forts which have been excavated. They were probably all inhabited and treated as refuges by the surrounding population. The houses discovered in them were round or rectangular and reconstructions of how they may have looked in Iron Age times can be seen at the Butser Ancient Farm in Hampshire. No ponds or wells have ever been found in these hilltop forts. We assume that maximum use was made of any rainwater that fell on the area or that people descended to the nearest stream.

We can be fairly sure that the hill forts were important centres, but we may never know how far their jurisdiction extended. Recent archaeological finds show that there were also lowland farms at this time, but these are not visible in the way that the hilltop enclosures are. The earliest inhabitants of the area were purely hunters and gatherers of fruit and other plant products. The only traces they left are stone implements, which you can view in the excellent local museums.

Gradually, Neolithic people incorporated farming into their activities. Some of this would leave no trace, but as time went on enclosures would have been necessary to contain livestock and mark boundaries between fields.

The associated patterns you will see on hillsides from time to time, if you are lucky enough to catch them in the right light, are the so-called 'Celtic' field systems. They show best where the vegetation is short or during droughts, and the best time to see them is in early morning and late evening.

The fields associated with prehistoric farming are not the broad level terraces which you will see alongside the Coast Path, particularly in Dorset. These terraces are medieval in origin, although they may overlie the 'Celtic' fields.

If you identify a criss-cross pattern of squares and rectangles much smaller than modern fields, between one-sixth of an acre and 1½ acres (0.07 to 0.6 hectares), you may be looking at evidence of some of the earliest farming in Britain.

We are fairly certain that such fields were used during the Iron Age, from 650 BC to the coming of the Romans, and it

The archway of Durdle Door, created by the action of waves beating against the limestone.

The cliffs of Swyre Head from Durdle Door.

would appear that Dorset farmers continued to use them during the Roman occupation.

We do not know if changes in customs during prehistoric times were the result of mass migrations of population, or of the influence of Britain's successful and powerful neighbours causing changes by more peaceful means.

We cannot be certain, therefore, whether the coastal hill forts were put up primarily by immigrants protecting themselves from a hostile local population, or whether the local population put them up to defend themselves from foreign invasion. Perhaps both happened at different periods of history.

From archaeological evidence we do know, however, that shortly before the coming of the Romans in AD 43 there were various trading establishments on the south coast of England. Inhabitants of Kent in particular were drinking wine and adopting other Roman fashions some time before the actual invasion took place. Hengistbury Head, a prominent landmark at Christchurch and clearly visible from the eastern end of this path, is known to have been a trading centre with Europe.

It is only with the coming of the Romans and the advent of written history that we can be more certain about what was going on at the time. It would seem that further east in England some of the tribes gave in to the Romans without major resistance.

However, the inhabitants of the area through which this path passes put up a very spirited resistance to the Roman invasion. The 'inland route' of the Coast Path in Dorset passes within walking distance of Britain's most spectacular Iron Age hill fort, Maiden Castle.

At the eastern entrance to this hill fort archaeologists have found evidence of a major battle. Most of the finds are well displayed and explained in the Dorset County Museum at Dorchester, and Maiden Castle is well worth a detour. At the complex eastern entrance, piles of sling stones from the Chesil Beach were found, as well as remains of the dead Britons massacred here. One of the bodies had a Roman ballista lodged through his spine.

We can conclude from this that the British defenders were not skilled in archery and relied on sling stones in their unsuccessful attempt to resist the efficient and well-armed Romans.

If you want to know more about this period I can thoroughly recommend museums in the towns through which you pass, as well as the Dorset County Museum.

11 Lulworth Cove to Kimmeridge

through the Lulworth Ranges
7 miles (11.2 km)

LULWORTH RANGE WALKS
LEGEND

Road open when range walks open
(Ref. SY881801 to SY895815)

Range Walks

Range Walk starting point

GENERAL INSTRUCTIONS

1. You must comply with the instructions of the wardens at all times.
2. You should not pick up any objects found on the range.
3. It is regretted that camping or fires are not allowed.
4. Please do not enter any building.
5. Please protect the wildlife. Do not collect specimens of flowers, birds, eggs, insects or fossils without permission.

For safety's sake please do not leave the paths and do not touch any ammunition you may see.

WARNING

All visitors to Lulworth Ranges must take heed that this is an Army Range and the public have no right of access when firing is taking place. Visitors must keep within the Way Marks on each path. If people stray away from the clearly visible path Way Marks they can endanger themselves and others because only the designated paths have been cleared of explosive. Paths are marked on both sides by plain wooden posts with yellow bands. They are placed at about 50 to 100 metre intervals and are clearly visible. In addition the boundaries of the coast path from Gold Down to Worbarrow Bay and from Flower's Barrow to Arish Mell to Bindon Hill are marked by a fence and yellow tipped posts.

DO NOT CROSS THESE FENCES.

The path 'A' to 'B' through the Lulworth Army Ranges (see pages 126–7) and the range walks are open to the public most weekends and school holidays. More information can be obtained by dialling 01929 404819 for a recorded message about opening times. Messages with specific queries may also be left. The exact routes of the walks may be changed from time to time.

Even if the range walks are closed, the road from East Lulworth to Steeple, 'C' to 'D', is often open in the evenings and on days when no firing is taking place on that particular part of the ranges. Signboards are posted on roads approaching the area and will indicate whether this road is open at the time. The road 'E' to 'F' is often open when all other roads through the ranges are closed. At times when the path 'A' to 'B', the East Lulworth–Steeple road, 'C' to 'D', and the East Lulworth–West Holme road, 'E' to 'F', are all closed, the walker will have to find a way of circumnavigating the whole of this area via Coombe Keynes, East Stoke, East Holme, Stoborough and Steeple.

Scale approx 1 inch to 1 mile

Contours are given in me
The vertical interval is

Contours are given in metres
The vertical interval is 10m

Scale approx 1 inch to 1 mile

The hard limestone bands of Mupe Rocks resist fierce storms, while the softer clays a

alk behind are washed away.

To get to the Fossil Forest from Lulworth Cove, and continue your walk eastwards, go down to the cove and turn left opposite the boathouse. Go up the steps behind the old boathouse, now a café. When you see the hotel swimming pool on your left follow the signs left high above the hotel through the scrub. When this emerges onto the open hill, turn sharp right to return to the clifftop path around the top of the cove's steep chalk cliffs.

The path descends to Little Bindon **65**, a small cottage once associated with the medieval monastery mentioned on page 76. The access to the Lulworth Army Ranges is immediately to the east of Little Bindon. Once inside the ranges, follow the boundary to the cliff top where you will see below you the Fossil Forest **66**.

Do not be disappointed by what you see. The round, bowl-like lumps of rock, some of which are hollow, once contained tree stumps of a forest which grew here perhaps 135 million years ago. The lumps of rock are the remains of the growths which formed round the trees. Further along you can see the ripple marks of an ancient beach.

These are the only fossil remains in this area. The Fossil Forest is a designated Site of Special Scientific Interest and the use of geological hammers in this area is illegal.

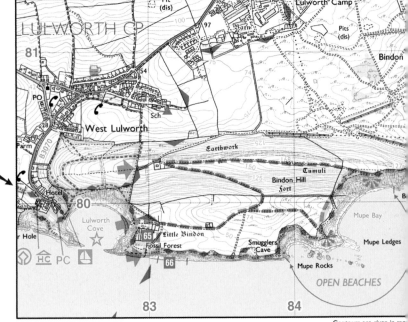

Beaches open only when ranges are open

Contours are given in me
The vertical interval is 5

About 800 yards after the Fossil Forest the path reaches Mupe Rocks and Mupe Bay. The path between Mupe and Kimmeridge Bays is almost immediately adjacent to the cliff top all the way. From Mupe Bay there is a stiff climb to the summit of Bindon Hill.

Now comes Arish Mell, a small shingle beach with chalk cliffs. There is no public access to the beach, which has not been cleared of explosives. A signed track leaves the Coast Path here to go to East Lulworth, Lulworth Castle and The Weld Arms pub. The path rises again steeply to the top of Rings Hill **67**, with its clifftop Iron Age hill fort called Flower's Barrow. From

ntours are given in metres
he vertical interval is 5m

Beaches open only when ranges are open

here the path descends very steeply to Worbarrow Bay, until 1943 a small fishing settlement.

Worbarrow Beach is open to the public when the range walks are open and it is safe for bathing. You can clamber up to the top of Worbarrow Tout for wonderful views of the surroundings. Just to the east of Worbarrow Tout is Pondfield with its fascinating marine wildlife.

For a display about the recent history of the Tyneham Valley, visit Tyneham Church **68**. The old village schoolroom has been restored to its 1920s layout and furnishing, giving a fascinating insight into those times. Tyneham has been uninhabited since 1943 but these two buildings have been restored. Buildings at Tyneham Farm are also being repaired

Beaches open only when ranges are open

Contours are given in met
The vertical interval is 5

and items relating to 1940s agricultural equipment and practice will be on display.

If you strike inland from Worbarrow along a track beside the stream and woods to visit Tyneham, you may return to the Coast Path directly at the top of Gad Cliff by a path which leads southwards from the village car park. If you need to press on eastwards, continue from Worbarrow Tout for a steep climb on to Gold Down and Gad Cliff.

Halfway along Gad Cliff you will pass the junction which leads up from Tyneham village, and then you will come to another junction where the Coast Path user must be careful to turn south-east towards Kimmeridge Bay for the descent. First of all this zig-zags down the slopes of Tyneham Cap, and then it rejoins the cliff edge, coming only slightly inland to take the short-cut across the headland of Broad Bench. The path then continues along the low black cliffs off Kimmeridge all the way to the Kimmeridge oil well **70**, which has been in production since 1957.

You are now outside the Army Ranges.

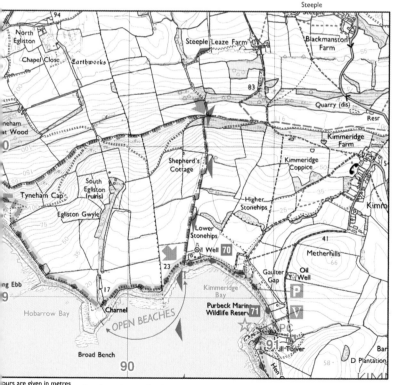

A CIRCULAR WALK AT TYNEHAM

See maps on pages 131 and 132
(see page 125 for details about Lulworth ranges and firing times)

Visits to Tyneham may only take place during Lulworth Range opening times – that is most weekends and school holidays. It is dangerous to enter the area at any other time. If in doubt, ring 01929 404819 for a recorded message about opening times. Messages with specific queries may also be left.

To walk to Tyneham start from the Whiteway Hill car park and picnic area **69** on the ridge overlooking Tyneham. Go through the wicket-gate west and carry on straight along the ridge, keeping between the yellow painted posts which define the area that has been cleared of explosives. Keep going until you reach the cliff top at Rings Hill, where you will find the massive embankments of Flower's Barrow, an Iron Age hill fort contemporary with many others along this coastline **67**. It is not certain whether this hill fort originally had ramparts on the seaward side; these may have been washed away in the succeeding 2,000 years. You can read more about these forts on page 120.

This first part of the walk is extremely easy, flat walking on short turf. The elderly or infirm should retrace their steps from the hill fort, having enjoyed outstanding views over the Tyneham Valley and towards St Aldhelm's Head in the east and the Isle of Portland in the west.

The next part of the walk calls for good walking shoes and caution, as it descends steep banks which can be very slippery.

Descend the Coast Path east until you come to Worbarrow Bay. Ahead is Worbarrow Tout. The beach is safe for bathing

Marine wildlife on the coast of Dorset and East Devon

While walking the Coast Path it is worth sparing some time to take a well-earned breather and explore the seashore, which exhibits excellent examples of most marine habitats.

The Dorset coast between Swanage and Weymouth provides the walker with the opportunity to experience the lower part of the shore, exposed for long periods on spring tides (following a new or full moon), owing to the rare phenomenon of a double low tide which affects this area.

and open during range walk opening times. From Worbarrow Tout turn inland up the Tyneham Valley along a flint track. One mile (1.6 km) inland the track turns sharply to the left into Tyneham car park and the deserted village of Tyneham.

In the church **68** there is a splendid display of photographs of the village as it was before the Army take-over in 1943. This was opened on the 60th anniversary of this event with a carol service in the church attended by the surviving inhabitants of the village, Worbarrow Bay and the farms and heathlands, at Christmas 2003.

Note also the expertly restored memorial to the Williams family in the north transept, the 13th-century piscina, the small and simple memorial to Elizabeth Tarrant on the north wall of the nave, and the Martin Travers window of the mother and child under a growing tree above the altar.

Just opposite the church is the old village schoolroom. This was in use until 1932 and all children of school age attended the same school, with a small platform at the eastern end being reserved for the infants. The schoolroom is equipped as it would have been in 1943, with wildlife statements in children's writing on each of the desks.

Buildings at Tyneham Farm are also being repaired and items of 1940s agricultural equipment and practice will be on display.

The wildlife of the Lulworth Army Ranges is unique because many parts of the area have never been affected by agricultural practices, which have changed the scenery so much elsewhere over the past 40 years.

Coming out of the schoolroom go to the right of the church through a gateway which leads to another steep track up to the top of the ridge, where you turn right for the Whiteway Hill car park **69**.

The keen-eyed Coast Path walker may notice that some species occur in abundance on Devon and West Dorset shores but are not found further east. The explanation is that such species, sea urchins are an example, are southern creatures associated with the Gulf Stream. The Dorset Wildlife Trust's Purbeck Marine Wildlife Reserve, the first of many in Britain, contains several seaweeds and animals which are at their easternmost limit in the Channel. Look out for the spectacular iridescent seaweed *Cystoseira tamariscifolia*, blue, purple or turquoise.

The deserted village of Tyneham, taken over by the Army in 1943.

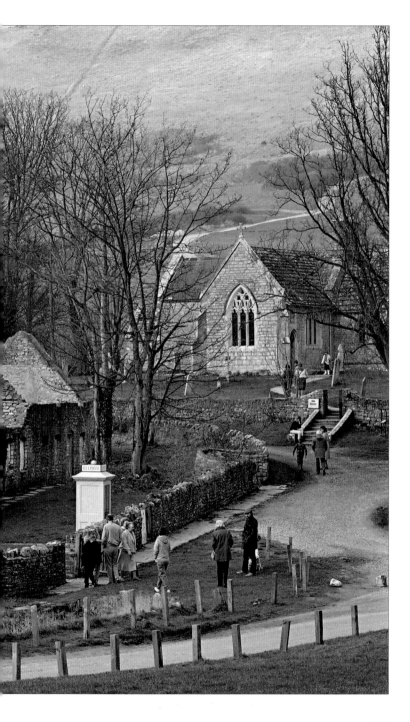

The aims of the reserve, which relies on voluntary co-operation, are to promote quiet enjoyment of the marine environment and to educate visitors about marine wildlife and its conservation. At Kimmeridge Bay, the main access point to the reserve, the reserve warden is on hand to show visitors the varied marine life and lead guided seashore walks. The Dorset Trust's information centre **71** (next to the slipway) contains a wildlife display and a rock pool aquarium.

At Kimmeridge you will see divers setting out in their inflatable boats to dive on the ledges and wrecks in the area, or to explore the Purbeck Marine Wildlife Reserve's underwater nature trail in Worbarrow Bay. The rocky ledges provide horizontal and vertical surfaces for plants and plant-like animals to colonise, and cracks and crevices for crabs, lobsters and fish to hide in. Wrecks are like artificial reefs and rich in wildlife.

Kimmeridge Bay is an excellent rocky shore to explore because of its clear water, rock pools and carpet of colourful seaweeds: bright green sea lettuce contrasts with the pink coralline weed and the holdfasts (anchors) of the large straplike kelps provide a refuge for many tiny animals – sea squirts, sea mats and brightly striped blue-rayed limpets. Beadlet and snakelocks anemones, bright yellow periwinkles, crabs and shrimps make up this rock pool world.

Other good rocky shores, well worth a detour, are Osmington Mills, Eype Mouth and the ledge between Charmouth and Lyme Regis. Check the tides before venturing out on to these ledges.

At first glance sandy shores, such as Studland and Charmouth, appear barren compared with rocky ones. On closer inspection, however, you can spot the signs of the animals which live buried in the sand: lugworm casts, sandmason tubes, meticulously built out of sand grains and shell fragments, empty shells and, if you are lucky, a masked crab, superbly camouflaged, hiding just beneath the sand surface.

Sand dunes consist of wind-blown sand trapped and stabilised by various hardy plants, such as the coarse marram grass. Older dune systems provide conditions in which a wide variety of plants, such as heathers, can grow.

The mudflats and saltmarsh areas of the sheltered shores of Poole Harbour, the Fleet and the Axe, Otter and Exe estuaries provide feeding grounds and roosting areas for wading birds, such as curlew, dunlin, redshank and oystercatcher, which probe the mud for worms and shellfish, and also grazing areas for ducks and geese. The Fleet, a brackish lagoon, tidal

This pair of spoonbills winter in Poole Harbour, preferring it to their normal locations in West Africa.

at the eastern end, contains vast beds of eelgrass, a favourite food of Brent geese and swans. The western margins of the Fleet can be visited from the Swannery, Abbotsbury, open in spring and summer.

Shingle is moved and deposited along the shore by waves and currents and is generally too unstable to support marine life. On the Chesil Bank, where the shingle has become stable at the top of the beach, specially adapted plants have colonised: sea pea, sea-kale, sea holly and yellow horned poppy. A section of the Chesil Bank is closed between 1 May and 31 August each year, the nesting season of the terns. There are many coastal and marine events and displays in the area. Contact local Tourist Information Centres for specific information about those that are planned to take place during your visit.

12 Kimmeridge to South Haven Point

past Worth Matravers and through Swanage to Poole
21 miles (33.7 km)

From the Kimmeridge oil well **70** the path keeps to the cliff top, passes to the seaward side of the row of cottages at Gaulter Gap, and then makes for the Clavel Tower **72** at the eastern end of the Bay. The beach is fascinating for its marine wildlife.

Among the boathouses under the Clavel Tower you find the Marine Centre of the Purbeck Marine Wildlife Reserve **71**. Entry is free. The centre is normally open when there are likely to be reasonable numbers of people. Guided walks often start here.

Contours are given in r
The vertical interval i

From the information centre, retrace your steps a short way up the road and then climb the flight of steps which leads past the Clavel Tower **72**, built as a folly in the 19th century and later used as a coastguard lookout. In 2008 the ruined tower was taken down and rebuilt further away from the crumbling cliffs and is now owned by the Landmark Trust as a holiday venue. The path now continues along the cliff edge for the next 2 miles (3 km). Beware particularly of crumbling cliffs on this section.

Between the Clavel Tower and Clavell's Hard, you may see traces of a cutting for the railway which used to take the shale down to a quay below the Clavel Tower.

On the ledges at Clavell's Hard you may be able to pick out the eight holes in the rock which took the posts supporting the small quay used to load barges with shale for export. 'Hard' means a place where boats can land, or a quay.

Next you pass Rope Lake Head **73**. Although this headland looks distinctive from a distance, it is difficult to tell when you are actually walking on it. The next section of the Coast Path remains just outside the field fences for 2 miles (3 km).

The path soon comes to Freshwater Steps **74**. Here there is a curious little headland with a man-made channel along the top of it and a waterfall at the end. The route branches just a few yards to the north to climb out of the Gwyle (the local name for a small valley) and then continues eastwards to rise steeply to the heights of Houns-tout Cliff.

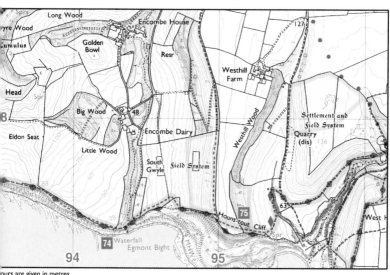

ours are given in metres
vertical interval is 5m

Houns-tout **75** is a very distinctive peak, capped with limestone, which is porous. This means that water which falls on the limestone filters through to the Kimmeridge shales below, which gradually become saturated, turning into a porridge-like, semi-fluid mass. From time to time these black layers flow out from under the limestone leaving it without support, and then thousands of tons of rock can cascade down the cliff and into the sea.

This process has accelerated rapidly in recent years. The path which descended to Chapman's Pool and then rose again on the other side has therefore been diverted up the valley to avoid danger. Please follow the signs carefully since the exact route may have been changed to avoid new falls since the time of writing.

The path at the bottom of the steep slope turns left and away from the sea over a stile, through a field, and over a causeway to cross a small stream. Turn right on to a surfaced road which keeps to the level of the contours for about $^3/_4$ mile (1.2 km). At Hill Bottom Cottage turn right and then right again over a small stream, through an iron bridlegate, and then fork left off the bridleway and up the hill. At the top of the small dry valley turn right on to the plateau of Emmet's Hill (*emmet* is dialect for ant).

Keep to the cliff top all the way along to Pier Bottom, where there is a dip and rise before you come back on to the top of the plateau to round the corner and come into sight of the Norman chapel of St Aldhelm **76**.

St Aldhelm was a Saxon Bishop of Sherborne, born before the middle of the 7th century. He was educated at Marlborough and Canterbury and later became the Abbot of Marlborough. He founded the monasteries at Frome in Somerset and Bradford-on-Avon in Wiltshire. When the diocese of Sherborne was formed, he became its first bishop. Bede wrote about St Aldhelm and commented on his writings. He was reputed to have spoken Latin and Greek as well as being able to read the Bible in Hebrew. He was popular in Wessex because of his use of the vernacular language as he preached to ordinary people.

The term St Alban's, used on the map and by the coastguard, is a misnomer but has gained common currency because the modern tongue finds St Aldhelm's difficult to pronounce.

It is possible that the 12th-century chapel, with its massive Norman vaults and buttress, may also have served at one time as a sea-mark.

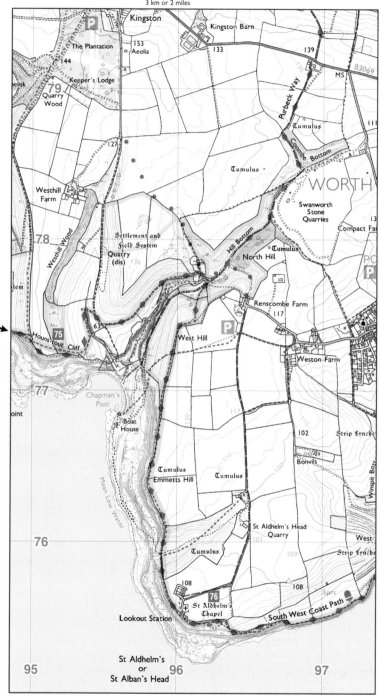

Corfe Castle
3 km or 2 miles

Kingston

Kingston Barn

P

The Plantation
153
Aeolia
133
139

144
B3069

Obelisk
79
Keeper's Lodge
MS

Quarry
Wood

Purbeck Way

127
Tumulus
111

Coombe Bottom

Westhill
Farm
Tumulus
WORTH

Swanworth
Stone
Quarries
Compact Far
13

78
Westhill Wood
Settlement and
Field System
Hill Bottom
Tumulus

Quarry
(dis)
136
North Hill

Renscombe Farm
117
PO
P

System
63.5
75
Houns-tout Cliff
Spr
West Hill
P

77
Chapman's
Pool
Weston Farm

Boat
House
102
Strip Lynche

Point
120
117
110

Tumulus
Emmetts Hill
Tumulus
100
Bonvils
90
110

76
St Aldhelm's Head
Quarry
101
109
West

Tumulus
Strip Lynche

Mean Low Water
108
108
Winspit Bot

76
St Aldhelm's
Chapel
Sprs

Lookout Station
South West Coast Path

95
96
97
St Aldhelm's
or
St Alban's Head

Contours are given in metres
The vertical interval is 5m

143

Structures which support it suggest that it once had a more substantial superstructure, which may have carried a light at night to guide sailors on their way. On the cliffs to the east of the coastguard lookout there is a monument commemorating radar research conducted here during the Second World War.

From St Aldhelm's Head to Swanage there will be few problems. Except for very slight detours inland to descend into hanging valleys at Winspit and Seacombe, the path stays adjacent to the field boundary next to the cliff all the way.

At St Aldhelm's Head you leave behind the magnificent views of Portland, Weymouth Bay, the chalk cliffs of Purbeck and the black cliffs of Kimmeridge shales, and come into view of the Isle of Wight and the solid limestone cliffs of Purbeck.

In spring puffins, razorbills and guillemots arrive to nest on the narrow ledges of these cliffs and rear their young, leaving again in late July for a lonely life many miles out to sea. You will also see fulmars, kittiwakes, shags, cormorants and black-backed gulls. The limestone downland flora and its associated wildlife here are quite outstanding. The National Trust now owns substantial stretches of these cliffs and manages the clifftop meadows in order to protect this flora.

A mile east of St Aldhelm's Head the route turns and goes about 100 yards inland before descending through a thicket to the Winspit Valley. Winspit is a small group of cliff quarries last worked during the Second World War. The old mines can be inspected safely from a distance, but do not venture within, because rocks can fall at any time and weigh many tons each.

East of Winspit the path rises behind the quarries and stays on the cliff top until Seacombe. This is a smaller rocky ledge, and the path detours round the back of the quarries here too.

From the back of the ledges at Seacombe Cliff the path strikes east along the cliff top. There are no problems following the path along this stretch and it soon comes to Headbury Quarry 77. Looking down you will see one of the cannons from the ship, the *Halsewell*, on its way to India when it was caught in a violent storm and destroyed at Halsewell Bars in 1786. One hundred and sixty-six people died, including the captain, his two daughters and two nieces.

The Coast Path continues along the cliff top to Dancing Ledge, with its small swimming pool cut into the rock by quarrymen at the beginning of the 20th century, while a stone sign set in the wall indicates a route north-east to Langton Matravers, where there are shops, a post office, pubs and camping sites.

98

99

tours are given in metres
e vertical interval is 5m

145

The path soon arrives at Durlston Country Park, where it stays on the cliff top to Anvil Point lighthouse **78**, built in 1881. The path then goes very close to the cliffs, giving superb views in spring of the seabirds below.

Then Durlston Castle comes into sight; this was a folly built by Mr Burt, a Swanage man who traded with London and brought many mementoes of London back as ballast after delivering stone. Around Swanage there are frequent reminders of this trade – bollards, the entire façade of the Swanage Town Hall (the Mercer's Hall from London) **80**, a clock-tower near the beach **81**, and countless other small items. He also built the castle, installed the enormous and fascinating limestone globe and had numerous inscriptions carved around the cliff top.

The castle is now a visitor centre for the Jurassic Coast. Go from the Globe to the seaward side of the castle to the main castle entrance and turn right along a shady walled track along the wooded clifftop towards Swanage. There should be spectacular views of the chalk cliffs to Old Harry rocks and the Needles on the Isle of Wight.

Follow this track until you see houses ahead of you and a path dipping to cross a stream, do not cross the stream but make a detour to avoid a massive landslip, going left and inland at the clearing in the woods with the curious stone seats. Turn right up Durlston Road and follow the gravel path on the grass verge.

As you see tall flats ahead of you and a path dipping to cross a stream, do not cross the stream but make a short detour to avoid a recent landslip by going left and inland at the clearing in the woods with the curious stone seats. When you get to Durlston Road there is a gravel path on the grass verge taking you right up

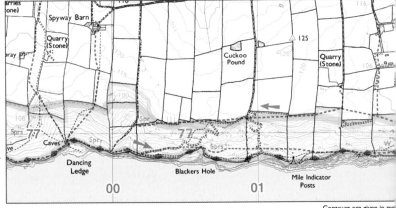

Contours are given in me
The vertical interval is 5

Ulwell Farm

Ulwell

Whitecliff Farm

South West Coast Path

FB

New Swanage

PC

Swanage Bay

Hotel

P

Groynes

SWANAGE

Swanage Railway

Cemy

Pier

DIVING SCHOOL

81

LB Sta

Peveril Point
Lookout Station

PC

82

80

Sch

Holiday
Park

Shafts

Townsend
Nature
Reserve

78

Durlston
Bay

California
Farm

South
Barn

Quarries
(stone)

Durlston

Durlston National
Nature Reserve

Durlston
Country
Park

79

P V PC

i

Durlston Head
Castle
Globe

Durlston Head

Round Down

South West Coast Path

77

78

Mile Indicator
Posts

Tilly Whim
Caves

Anvil Point

03

04

contours are given in metres
the vertical interval is 5m

147

the road. Turn right into Belle Vue Road to a path going right onto the open green lawns of Peveril Point. You are now a stone's throw from all the many delights of Swanage.

Swanage town is worth exploring. Near the junction of Durlston Road and Belle Vue Road you may have seen a water tower built in the same mock-Gothic style as Durlston Castle. If you are interested in industrial archaeology you may wish to look at it more closely. Down below in the centre the mill pond, the lock-up ('for the punishment of wickedness and vice') behind the town hall **80**, and the Tythe Barn Museum **82** are all worth a visit. If you have time you can take a short return steam train ride on the Swanage Railway, travelling in 1950s' style, to the magnificent hill-top Norman castle and the village of Corfe Castle.

To get to Studland follow the sea front northwards to the end. Then either, tide permitting, walk along the beach here to rejoin the path up a small gully at the end of the Groynes, or go

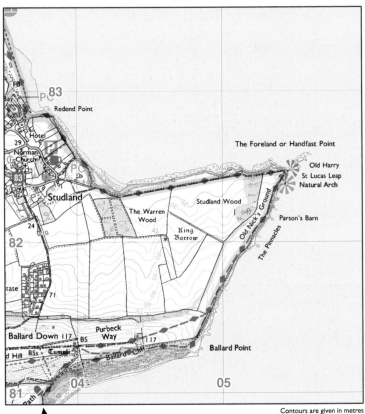

Contours are given in metres
The vertical interval is 5m

The chalk cliffs of the Pinnacles, typical of the spectacular scenery to be found along this coastline.

up the Studland road some 800 yards north-west of its junction with the sea front. Follow Ulwell Road up the hill from the end of the sea front, go to the right of the church, carrying straight on up the hill along Redcliffe Road. At the corner shop turn right into Ballard Way and waymarks then take you back along a private road (public footpath) through the Ballard Estate. Between nos. 22 and 24 there is a short path through to the clifftop lawns. At the northern end of the lawns follow some steps to cross a small valley, where you meet the path from the beach. The path continues northwards outside the fence to Ballard Down (steep rise) and then inside the fence to the top of the Down. At the top cross the stile and follow the cliff top to the dramatic white chalk stacks of Old Harry (NT). Keep parallel to the cliff through a coppice and some open fields. As you near the first house, follow the path going towards the cliff to the seaward side of the garden. Walk along the beach past the huts. Between the last few huts there is a set of steps leading to the cliff top. Turn right at the top of the cliff and follow the edge past the WWII Fort Henry guarding the entrance to Studland Bay and Poole Harbour, through the woodland to Middle Beach. Follow the beach to the blue marker celebrating the end of the South West Coast Path at South Haven Point **84**, where you may wish to have your photograph taken.

If you decide to go through Studland village there are shops, car parks, a pub, and access to sandy beaches and the nature reserve. The tiny church of St Nicholas **83** may have been built shortly before the Norman Conquest, with the nave being rebuilt in the 11th century, some 12th-century alterations, and only minor changes to the structure since that date. You can go along the village lanes until you follow a sign saying Middle Beach car park. Leave the car park to your left and descend the track to the beach. From here to South Haven Point is nearly 3 miles (4 km) of walking on soft sandy beach. It can be hard going, although it is easier near the waterline. The National Trust has also waymarked a way through the dunes, the Heather Walk, with yellow-topped posts, which you may follow as an alternative.

From the far side of the chain ferry which takes you to Sandbanks there is another ferry, at hourly intervals in the summer, to Brownsea Island (NT) **85**. There are walks around the island and guided visits to the nature reserve **86** most afternoons.

You have reached the end of the South West Coast Path and are now officially in Southern England.

Pontoons
Landing Stages

Harley Wood
Church Hill
Farm Buildings
Piers
Branksea Castle
Landing Stages

85
86

24 W

MHW

Harry Point

North Haven Point

Ferry P (Summer)

Hotel

Stone Island

PC

P
Groynes

87

84
2

South Haven Point

Gravel Point

FB

South West Coast Path

Shell Bay

Toll

PC
P

Dunes

Jerry's Point

Bramble Bush Bay

FB

86

Stone Island Lake

Redhorn Lake

Dunes

MHW

MLW

Redhorn Quay

's Bay

ND CP

Studland Heath

sland

85

ad Point

Ferry Road

Little Sea

Studland Bay

84

Studland and Godlingston Heath National Nature Reserve

Sewage Works

Salterne

Pipley Bridge

V

PC

02
03
12
04

Knoll House

Contours are given in metres
The vertical interval is 5m

151

A CIRCULAR WALK FROM KIMMERIDGE BAY

5 miles (7.8 km) (see maps on pages 140–41)

From Rope Lake Head **73** there is a permissive path, which the local farmer and landowner invite you to use, to get to Swyre Head. Should you wish to return to Kimmeridge from Swyre Head you can follow a bridleway along the top of the ridge, with magnificent views of the surrounding coastal scenery in both directions. The bridleway joins a track, an unsurfaced country road, and you cross the road which leads down to Kimmeridge to reach the path down to Kimmeridge Church. From the churchyard entrance follow the farm track through Kimmeridge Farm and then tak the public footpath, which more or less keeps in the valley parallel with the stream to Gaulter Gap.

A CIRCULAR WALK AT WORTH MATRAVERS

2½ miles (4 km) (see map on page 145)

The village of Worth Matravers has a pub (The Square and Compass), a post office and two tea shops, one with a small museum. The church has a Norman archway and is worth a visit. If you have the chance to take one of the guided walks around the village, its fascinating past, including tales of the infamous smuggler Gulliver, as well as the story of Nonconformist worship in the village blacksmith's, will be revealed.

There is a regular bus service from Swanage to Worth Matravers, or a car park situated to the north of the village. The bus will leave you on the village green but, from the car park, make your way seawards, leaving The Square and Compass to your left, and you will come into sight of the village green. From the green make your way towards the coast by following the signs for Seacombe next to the bus stop. Go a few yards down a small track giving access to houses, and then turn left along a very narrow path between houses, emerging into a field full of 'strip lynchets' – these were the fields of medieval England.

Go straight across the valley and cross the stone wall by the stile. Keep straight on across the fields until you drop into the Seacombe Valley and then follow the stream down to the sea. To return, turn right (west) at the end of the valley and after ¾ mile (1.2 km) the Coast Path brings you to the quarries and rock ledges of Winspit. Turn inland, keeping right at the junction by the treatment works, and you will arrive back at the village green.

Puffins still breed in very small numbers on the Purbeck coast around Dancing Ledge, and at Portland Bill, but the colonies may become extinct quite soon if the current downward trend is allowed to continue.

A CIRCULAR WALK AT DURLSTON

6¾ miles (10.8 km) (see maps on pages 145–47)

If you are based at Swanage you can walk an upper path from the information centre at Durlston Country Park **79**, returning via the Coast Path.

From the information centre, cross Round Down, keeping to the higher part of the ridge above the 'weirs', the local name for the steep slopes leading down to the sea. A public footpath then follows along the top of the weirs all the way to Dancing Ledge.

To the west of that point the National Trust and a private landowner allow the public to use a continuation, which is clearly signed and leads all the way along the top of the steeper slopes to Seacombe Valley. Descend the Seacombe Valley and return by the Coast Path to Durlston Head and Swanage.

Brownsea Castle, Poole Harbour. The view from the end of your walk. Henry VIII built a castle here; later wealthy owners built this one, now used by John Lewis staff for leisure breaks. Brownsea Island, famous for the first ever Scout camp as well as for its varied wildlife, has a ferry service from April to October.

Coastal mining and quarrying

The Coast Path between Exmouth and Poole passes countless quarries. Many of the small quarries were for the extraction of chalk and limestone which fed the large number of lime kilns along the route. If you do the circular walk at Branscombe you will also have seen the copper ore (malachite) quarries above Street, and at Beer you may visit the chalk quarries which produced building stone from the very hard chalk layers there.

One village which is particularly beautiful because of the use of local stone is Abbotsbury. Here the limestone has a large iron content and is therefore a beautiful golden yellow.

The villages which lie to the south of the ridgeway route behind Weymouth are built of a light grey limestone, 'Ridgeway stone', and many of the churches and smaller manor houses of South Dorset are also built from this material. The coastal villages all the way along are built of stone which would have been quarried locally from the nearest hillside but rarely, if ever, exported.

Stone for the cathedrals and cities of England

The exception is in Portland and Purbeck. Here the building stone has been exported since Roman times. The ready access to the sea meant that the stone was easy to export, and it can be seen in medieval cathedrals throughout England and France, in particular the green-black Purbeck 'marble' mined here for the dark columns you may notice in Norman and early English cathedrals.

From the quarries and mines the stone was lowered into barges with derricks called 'whims' and taken to Swanage, and you may be able to trace some of the anchor points for the derricks. With the tourist industry now bringing wealth once again to Britain's historical cities and monuments, the local quarries just inland are thriving and proudly continue a tradition of nearly 2,000 years.

The Tythe Barn Museum in Swanage has a display about quarrying. If you follow the paths between Swanage and Worth Matravers, you will see quarrymen working the stone.

Clay for the Staffordshire potteries

In 1820, 20,000 tons of clay a year were being shipped to Liverpool, and that one-third of the pottery made in England by the middle of the 19th century was made from Poole clay.

The clay came from the southern shores of Poole harbour, and still does, and in the 19th century it was taken to quays on the headlands, tipped into 50-ton barges and transferred at Poole into seagoing ships. It has also been used locally for many centuries, and manufacture still goes on at Poole Pottery.

Gaslights for Paris

In the bands of shale at Kimmeridge there is a 2-foot (60-centimetre) layer of the bituminous shale known as 'black stone' or 'Kimmeridge coal'. At various times it has been used as a fuel for industry. In the 17th century it was quarried to fuel an alum works and the alum was used for dyeing, printing and tanning.

Later a glass works was built at the Bay and this was excavated some years ago.

During the 19th century an attempt was even made to supply the gasworks of Paris with Kimmeridge shale for Parisian street lighting. The contract fell through, however. One wonders whether the penetrating sulphurous smell deterred the Parisians. Local people used it to heat their houses right up until the 19th century.

The Romans used the shale to make ornaments, armlets and rings. Decorative chair legs made from the shale are in the County Museum at Dorchester and there is evidence that Iron Age people boiled sea water, using the shale as fuel, in order to manufacture salt. The salt-boiling works probably lie deep beneath the mounds of shale beside the cliff at Clavel Tower.

Oil for the 21st century

The search for oil has covered the whole of the area through which the Coast Path passes. The first drillings were unsuccessful, but as techniques improved and drills could go deeper, so more oil has been discovered.

The well at Kimmeridge Bay **70** has been operating since the late 1950s with a small but steady output. Then, some 20 years later, Wytch Farm oilfield on the southern shores of Poole harbour was discovered. Engineers have been at work there since the late 1970s, and after 1980 crude oil was pumped out at a rate of up to 4,000 barrels per day and exported by train on part of the old Swanage Railway. Most of this oil has come from the 'Bridport reservoir', which is a relatively shallow deposit.

With the discovery of the Sherwood reservoir, at a much deeper level, there has been an increase in production to 100,000 barrels per day. This makes it the largest on-shore oilfield in Europe. Liquid gas is exported by road, and oil goes by pipeline to the Solent.

The installations have been carefully sited to cause the minimum disturbance to wildlife, and carefully hidden so that it is difficult to see them at all. In recognition of this the project has won a Civic Trust award, the Queen's Award for Environmental Achievement, and many others.

PART THREE

USEFUL INFORMATION

Websites

The official website giving information on the entire South West Coast Path is www.national trail.co.uk/southwestcoastpath

This is a comprehensive information source and incorporates the latest news about the Path and links to travel and accommodation information.

The South West Coast Path Association, www.southwestcoastpath.org.uk, has news on the latest developments.

The Dorset and East Devon World Heritage Site: www.jurassiccoast.com

For countryside-related government organisations go to: www.naturalengland.org.uk

Geological information: http://content.swgfl.org.uk/jurassic

Transport

The Department of Transport website www.transportdirect.info/TransportDirect/en/ allows you to compare journey times for different modes of transport and has the latest information on roadworks.

Detailed information about all journeys by public transport in the UK is available from the Traveline 0871 200 22 33 or online at www.traveline.org.uk

Rail

www.nationalrail.co.uk/planmyjourney
www.southwesttrains.co.uk/
www.firstgreatwestern.co.uk
www.crosscountrytrains.co.uk

There are regular and frequent services to Exeter from all parts of Britain via London Waterloo, London Paddington, Bristol or Westbury. Change at Exeter St David's. From there to Exmouth there are half-hourly services Monday to Saturday, rather less frequently on Sundays in winter.

The last stretch is usually in small diesel railcars from which you get fine views of the Exe Estuary. If you are not in too much of a hurry, it is well worth stopping at Topsham and Lympstone. For details see Crossing the Exe, page 22.

There are half-hourly South West Trains services from London Waterloo to Poole and Weymouth, and daily Arriva Cross Country and First Great Western through services, avoiding London, to most parts of the country. Booking is not normally required for South West Trains services.

For European visitors, international services from Brussels, from Northern Europe, and Paris, from Southern Europe via the Channel Tunnel, arrive at St Pancras International in London and take less than three hours from city centre to city centre. Take the Northern Line to Waterloo for direct express services to Exeter, Weymouth, Bournemouth or Poole for access to the beginning, middle or end of this section of the path. Advance fares, booked online or at stations up to three months/twelve weeks ahead, are generally cheaper than air, but more than bus/coach travel. For timetable and fare enquiries, go to www.thetrainline.com or telephone 0871 200 22 33.

Swanage Railway gives a 1950s-style ride from Swanage to Norden (where there is a park-and-ride) and back with classic steam locomotives: 01929 425800; www.swanagerailway.co.uk

Buses

www.nationalexpress.com

Daily express coaches run from all parts of the country to all the coastal towns. Tel. 08717 818181. The Jurassic Coast bus, Coastlink X53 service, runs from Exeter to Wareham, stopping at Lyme, Charmouth, Bridport, West Bay, Abbotsbury and Weymouth. www.firstgroup.com/ ukbus/ for timetable.

There are services in the Exmouth–Lyme Regis sector, with buses using the main road which is never far from the coast, and regular stops at all the coastal towns along the route. The Weymouth–Axminster hourly service no. 31 via Dorchester, Bridport, Morecombelake (Golden Cap) and Lyme Regis is useful for the Lyme–Bridport section.

Coastal villages off the A35 in West Dorset have only very intermittent services, or none at all, as do Lulworth and Kimmeridge.

Worth Matravers, Langton, Swanage and Studland have regular services with connections to Wareham and Poole, with stops close to the railway stations.

For enquiries contact the following: www.traveline.org.uk – for all route planning on public transport in the UK.
www.firstgroup.com/ukbus/south west/devon/home/
Wilts and Dorset Bus Company Ltd, Arndale Centre, Poole.
01202 673555
(Swanage–Studland–Poole);
www.wdbus.co.uk
Swanage Bus Station. Tel. 01929 422528.

Devon General Bus Station, Belgrave Road, Exeter, EX1 2LB Tel. 01392 427711.

There may be special 'Explorer' tickets available from these firms, which are good value and useful when walking in the area.

Ferries

The Starcross Ferry runs an hourly service, seven days a week, from May to October. It leaves Starcross hourly from 10.40am to 4.40pm with an additional last ferry at 5.40pm May to September, 6.15pm in August. It leaves Exmouth for Starcross hourly from 10.10am to 4.10pm, with an additional last ferry at 5.10pm in May to October, 6.00pm in August. Access to the ferry is through Starcross Station, www.exe2sea.co.uk/ferry.shtml.

The Studland Chain Ferry runs a frequent daily service from early morning to late evening, with a break in late autumn for maintenance.

Contact the following for further information:
Exe Water Taxi Service operates from 8am–6pm, April–end of October, on request in person from the Exmouth side, or by hailing from the Dawlish Warren side on 07970 918418 or by phoning in advance on 01392 873409. The Starcross Ferry (Starcross to Exmouth), Starcross Pier and Ferry Co., 26 Marine Parade, Dawlish. Tel. 01626 862452.
The Fleet Observer – explore the underwater world of the Fleet lagoon in a glass-bottomed boat. Six sailings a day operated by the Chesil Bank and Fleet Nature Reserve until September. Tel. 01305 759692. www.thefleetobserver.co.uk
Bournemouth–Swanage Motor Road and Ferry Co., Floating Bridge, Sandbanks, Poole, Dorset. Tel. 01929 450203.

Accommodation

Finding accommodation in the peak holiday period is not easy, especially for single nights – booking in advance is recommended.

The most comprehensive listing of walker-friendly accommodation is maintained by Luggage Transfers Ltd in conjunction with the South West Coast Path Association. This can be found on the website www.luggagetransfers.co.uk and is included in the annually updated guidebook produced by the South West Coast Path Association. The guidebook is available from many bookshops, and is free with membership to the Association.

Youth Hostels and campsites are noted on the Ordnance Survey maps in this guide, and many additional campsites spring up during the summer. The solitary backpacker may be able to camp in a farmer's field, but permission should always be obtained first. For details of all Youth Hostels visit www.yha.org.uk. A centralised telephone booking service is available on 0870 241 2314.

There are also a number of independent hostels – an annual guide is published by the Backpackers Press, 01629 580427, or visit www.independenthostelguide.co.uk/ for details or to email hostels directly.

A list of Tourist Information Centres (TICs) is given below; they will answer enquiries about accommodation, including camping. It is best to approach the TIC nearest to the place you wish to stay. Note that not all TICs are open throughout the year. Most operate a 'book a bed ahead' service for personal callers for the same or the next night. A fee is charged but will be deducted from your bill by the accommodation provider.

Tourist Information Centres

The following information centres are affiliated to the West Country Tourist Board, 60 St David's Hill, Exeter, Devon EX4 4QS.

From east to west

The Tourist Information Centre, Alexandra Terrace, Exmouth, Devon EX8 1NZ. Tel. 01395 222299. www.exmouthguide.co.uk

The Tourist Information Centre, Fore Street, Budleigh Salterton, Exeter, Devon EX9 6NG. Tel. 01395 445275 www.eastdevon.net/tourism

The Tourist Information Centre, The Esplanade, Ham Lane, Sidmouth, Exeter, Devon EX10 8XR. Tel. 01395 516441.

The Tourist Information Centre, Underfleet, Seaton, Devon EX12 2TB. Tel. 01297 21660. www.eastdevon.net/tourism/seaton

The Tourist Information Centre, The Old Courthouse, Church Street, Axminster EX13 5AQ. Tel. 01297 34386.

The Tourist Information Centre, Guildhall Cottage, Church Street, Lyme Regis, Dorset DT7 3BS. Tel. 01297 442138. www.dorsetforyou.com www.lymeregistourism.co.uk

The Tourist Information Centre, 47 South Street, Bridport, Dorset DT6 3NY. Tel. 01308 424901. www.westdorset.com

The Tourist Information Centre, The King's Statue, The Esplanade, Weymouth, Dorset DT4 7AN. Tel. 01305 785747. www.weymouth.gov.uk or www.resort-guide.co.uk/weymouth.html

The western boundary of the Southern Tourist Board is at Weymouth and its address is: 40 Chamberlayne Road, Eastleigh, Hampshire S050 5JH. Tel. 023 8062 5400.

The only centre in this area which the Coast Path user will pass directly is at Swanage and the address is: Tourist Information Centre, Shore Road, Swanage, Dorset BH19 1LB. Tel. 01929 422885. www.swanage.gov.uk

Coastal Visitor Centres

Charmouth Heritage Coast Centre 01297 560772

Chesil Beach Centre 01305 760579

Kimmeridge Marine Centre 01929 481044

Lulworth Heritage Centre 01929 400587

Lyme Regis Marine Aquarium 01297 444230

Lyme Regis Museum 01297 443370

Portland Tourist Information Centre 01305 861233

Studland Beach Information Centre 01929 450259

Swanage Heritage Centre 01929 421427

Baggage carrying and packaged walking holidays

Several firms operate guided or unguided holidays along sections of the South West Coast Path. A link to a current list of operators recommended by the West Country Tourist Board will be found on the Accommodation page of the official South West Coast Path website, www.southwestcoastpath.com

Getting your bags carried between your overnight stops is easy. Luggage Transfers Ltd moves thousands of walkers bags along the Coast Path each year. To find out more visit their website at www.luggagetransfers.co.uk, where you can also find a comprehensive listing of walker-friendly accommodation close to the path.

Guided Walks

There are many guided walks along the route of the Path, led by local experts and adding a completely new dimension to a holiday on this coast. The normal duration is a couple of hours. Between Easter and October copies of the programmes may be obtained from Tourist Information Centres, Heritage Coast information centres, public libraries and museums. Some are organised privately and others by local civic and naturalists' societies, and by the Jurassic Coast World Heritage Site Team, East Devon AONB Service, Dorset AONB Service and the National Trust.

Local organisations

You may like to join, or make a contribution or donation to, one of the local organisations which helps to look after the coast.

Devon Wildlife Trust, Cricklept Mill, Commercail Road, Exeter EX2 4AB. Tel. 01392 279244. www.devonwildlifetrust.org

Dorset Wildlife Trust, Brooklands Farm, Forston, Dorchester DT2 7AA. Tel. 01305 264620. www.dorsetwildlifetrust.org.uk

Dorset Natural History and Archaeological Society, Dorset County Museum, High West Street, Dorchester DTI 1XA. Tel. 01305 262735.

Dorset Countryside Volunteers 01305 889728. www.dcv.org.uk

Other useful addresses

National Trust, Devon Regional Office, Killerton House, Broadclyst, Exeter EX5 3LE. Tel. 01392 881691. www.nationaltrust.org.uk/

National Trust, Wessex, Eastleigh Court, Bishopstrow, Warminster, Wilts BA12 9HW. Tel. 01985 843 600

Natural England, National Trails team, Block B Government Buildings, Whittington Road, Worcester WR5 2LQ www.nationaltrail.co.uk

Ordnance Survey, Adanac Drive, Southampton SO16 0AS. Tel. 0845 605 0505. www.ordnancesurvey.co.uk

The Ramblers, 2nd Floor, Camelford House, 87–90 Albert Embankment, London SE1 7TW. Tel. 020 7339 8500. www.ramblers.org.uk

The South West Coast Path Association, Liz Wallis, Administrator, South West Coast Path Association, Bowker House, Lee Mill Bridge, Ivybridge, Devon, PL21 9EF. Tel. 01752 896237. Email: info@swcp.org.uk. This is the best site for the latest information on the route.

South West Coast Path Team, c/o Devon County Council, Matford Lane Offices, Exeter EX2 4QW. Tel. 01392 383560. swcpteam@devon.gov.uk Co-ordinates the management of the Souh West Coast Path.

Nearby places of interest

Exeter cathedral, museum, Georgian houses.

East Budleigh Raleigh's birthplace, interesting village and church with many Raleigh reminders.

Otterton Mill working mill open to the public, with corn-grinding demonstrations, stone-ground flour and home-made bread for sale, tea rooms.

Bicton Gardens formal gardens of an early 18th-century stately home which is now an agricultural college.

Sidmouth Regency and Victorian buildings of style and elegance, and museum.

Bovey House now a hotel and restaurant, 1 mile (1.6 km) north of Beer, built in 1592 with Jacobean carvings in hall and dining room and a Restoration ceiling in the King Charles Room.

Seaton Axe Valley Heritage Museum above Town Hall; Seaton Tramway.

Forde Abbey fine house and gardens based on medieval abbey.

Lyme Regis Town Mill, 01297 443579, restored water mill on the Lym, a few hundred yards upstream from The Pilot Boat Inn. Refreshments, exhibitions, guided tours. www.townmill.org.uk Lyme Regis Museum www.lymeregismuseum.co.uk

Charmouth Charmouth Heritage Coast Centre www.charmouth.org. Excellent geological information and starting point for guided walks. 01297 560772

Upwey the Wishing Well, ancient monument. Tea rooms, source of the River Wey, gardens.

Dorchester Old Crown Court where the Tolpuddle Martyrs were tried, Roman town house, the walks which surround the town on the line of the Roman ramparts, Roman amphitheatre, riverside walks, medieval churches, County Museum with displays on prehistory and Roman mosaics. Max Gate, Hardy's house, is open. Ask local TIC or see NT handbook for times.

Wolfeton House within walking or cycling distance of Dorchester. Small, intriguing manor house.

Wareham Saxon ramparts complete, two medieval churches, one Saxon or early Norman, and one with very early Christian inscriptions. Quay on River Frome and some fine old town houses.

Corfe Castle (NT) Purbeck stone village and massive Norman fortress which played an important role in many episodes of English history. Can be reached by vintage railway trains by the Swanage Railway, highly recommended.

Studland important heathland nature reserves managed by Nature Conservancy Council. Solid and beautiful Norman village church. Miles of sandy beaches.

Bibliography

Austen, Jane, *Persuasion* (Chatto & Windus, and Penguin, 1970).

Barns, Norman, *The East Devon Way: A walker's inland route from the Exe to the Lym* (East Devon District Council, 1993).

Bond, Lilian, *Tyneham, A Lost Heritage* (Dovecote Press, 1984).

Bulloch, John, and Miller, Henry, *Spy Ring, The Full Story of the Portland Naval Spy Case* (Martin Secker & Warburg, London, 1961). The story of the spy-ring that worked at the Underwater Weapons Establishment at Southwell and the Portland naval base, run by the Soviets through the 1950s to spy on the progress of the western anti-submarine technology.

Burnett, David, *Dorset Shipwrecks* (Dovecote Press, 1982).

Butler, Richard (ed.), *A View from the Cliffs* (Devon Books). A guide to the East Devon Heritage Coast.

Chaffey, John, *The Dorset and East Devon Coast* (Jurassic Coast World Heritage Site) (Dorset Books, 2003).

Coxe, A. Hippisley, *Smuggling in the West Country* (Tabb House, 1984).

Cullingford, Cecil, *A History of Dorset* (Phillimore & Co., 1980).

Draper, Jo, *Dorset: The Complete Guide* (Dovecote Press).

Falkner, J. M., *Moonfleet* (Puffin, 1994).

Fowles, John, *A Short History of Lyme Regis* (Dovecote Press, 1982).
— *The French Lieutenant's Woman* (Jonathan Cape, 1969, and Vintage, 2009).
— and Draper, Jo, *Thomas Hardy's England* (Jonathan Cape, 1984).

Hardy, Thomas, *The Trumpet Major, The Well-Beloved* (set on Portland) and other novels.

Hoyt, Edwin P., *The Invasion before Normandy* (Robert Hale, London, 1993). An account of Exercise Tiger, just before D-Day, in which hundreds of American servicemen died off Portland Bill/West Bay, kept secret for several decades after WWII.

Hyland, Paul, *Isle of Purbeck – Discover Dorset* series, (Dovecote Press, Wimborne BH21 4JD).

Kay-Robinson, Denys, *The Landscape of Thomas Hardy* (Webb & Bower, 1984).

The National Trust Coast of Devon (Devon Books).

Legg, Rodney, *The Jurassic Coast* (Dorset Publishing Company 2002 and 2003).

Lewis, Nigel, *Channel Firing, the Tragedy of Exercise Tiger* (Harbour Books, Dartmouth, 1994).

Morris, Stuart, *Portland – Discover Dorset* series, (Dovecote Press).

Pitfield, F. P., *Purbeck Parish Churches* (Dorset Publishing Co., 1981).

Pomeroy, Colin, *Castles and Forts – Discover Dorset* series, (Dovecote Press).

Royal Commission for Historical Monuments, *Dorset* (8 vols, HMSO, 1952 and 1970).

Sanctuary, A., *Rope, Twine and Net Making* (Shire Publications, 1980).

Stanier, Peter, *The Industrial Past – Discover Dorset* series, (Dovecote Press, 1998).

Thomas, Jo, *Stone Quarrying – Discover Dorset* series, (Dovecote Press).

Wallington, Mark, *500 Mile Walkies* (Hutchinson/Arrow, 1986).

Wilkinson, Gerald, *Woodland Walks in South West England* (OS and Webb & Bower, 1986).

The Official Guide to the Jurassic Coast, A Walk through Time, may be ordered from www.jurassiccoast.com

There is also a leaflet on the Jurassic Coast and one on the South West Coast Path available at TICs.

See also www.nationaltrail.co.uk

Ordnance Survey Maps covering the South West Coast Path (Exmouth to Poole)

Landranger Maps 192, 193, 194, 195.

Explorer and Outdoor Leisure Maps

115 Exmouth & Sidmouth

116 Lyme Regis & Bridport

OL 15, Purbeck and South Dorset covers the rest of the area at 1:25 000.

The Official Guides to all of

Cotswold Way
Anthony Burton

100 miles of quintessentially
English landscape

ISBN 978 1 84513 519 5

Cleveland Way
Ian Sampson

Over 100 miles of magnificent
walking on the North York Moors

ISBN 978 1 84513 520 1

Hadrian's Wall Path
Anthony Burton

Follow the Roman Wall
from coast to coast

ISBN 978 1 84513 567 6

Yorkshire Wolds Way
Roger Ratcliffe

A superbly tranquil walk through the
unspoilt chalk hills of East Yorkshire

ISBN 978 1 84513 643 7

**Pembrokeshire
Coast Path**
Brian John

180 miles of clifftop, beach and cove
around the magnificent Welsh coast

ISBN 978 1 84513 602 4

South Downs Way
Paul Millmore

100 miles of glorious chalk downland
for the walker, cyclist and horse rider

ISBN 978 1 84513 565 2

Pennine Way
NORTH: Bowes to Kirk Yetholm
Tony Hopkins

140 miles of magnificent walking
through remote countryside

ISBN 978 1 84513 562 1

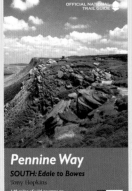

Pennine Way
SOUTH: Edale to Bowes
Tony Hopkins

140 miles of wild country on
Britain's oldest long-distance path

ISBN 978 1 84513 639 0

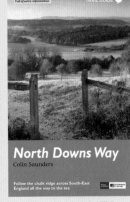

Completely rewritten
Full of extra information

North Downs Way
Colin Saunders

Follow the chalk ridge across South-East
England all the way to the sea

ISBN 978 1 84513 677 2

Britain's National Trails

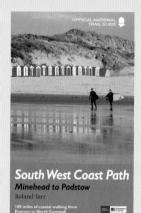

South West Coast Path
Minehead to Padstow
Roland Tarr

160 miles of coastal walking from
Exmoor to North Cornwall

ISBN 978 1 84513 640 6

South West Coast Path
Padstow to Falmouth
John Macadam

From golden beaches to rugged coves
around Britain's southernmost tip

ISBN 978 1 84513 641 3

Thames Path
David Sharp

Follow England's river all the way from its
peaceful source into the heart of the capital

ISBN 978 1 84513 566 9

South West Coast Path
Falmouth to Exmouth
Brian Le Messurier

172 miles of dramatic coves, cliffs and
beaches from Cornwall to Devon

ISBN 978 1 84513 564 5

South West Coast Path
Exmouth to Poole
Roland Tarr

From Jane Austen's Cobb to Lulworth Cove
– over 100 miles of historic coastline

ISBN 978 1 84513 642 0

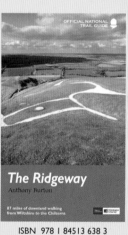

The Ridgeway
Anthony Burton

87 miles of downland walking
from Wiltshire to the Chilterns

ISBN 978 1 84513 638 3

ISBN 1 85410 957 X

Peddars Way and
Norfolk Coast Path
Bruce Robinson

90 miles from Breckland to
salt marsh and sea cliffs

ISBN 978 1 84513 570 6

Offa's Dyke Path
SOUTH: Chepstow to Knighton
Ernie and Kathy Kay and Mark Richards

Follow the ancient earthwork up the Wye
Valley and alongside the Black Mountains

ISBN 978 1 84513 561 4

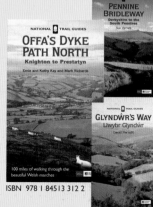

PENNINE
BRIDLEWAY
Derbyshire to the
South Pennines
Sue Viccars

OFFA'S DYKE
PATH NORTH
Knighton to Prestatyn
Ernie and Kathy Kay and Mark Richards

100 miles of walking through the
beautiful Welsh marches

ISBN 978 1 84513 312 2

GLYNDWR'S WAY
Llwybr Glyndwr
David Perrott

ISBN 1 85410 968 5

Definitive guides to Britain's most popular long-distance walks

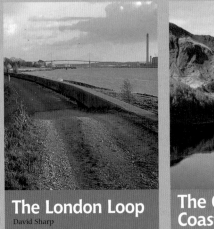

The London Loop
David Sharp

The walker's M25 – over 140 miles of footpaths in London's secret countryside

ISBN 978 1 84513 521 8

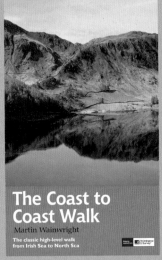

The Coast to Coast Walk
Martin Wainwright

The classic high-level walk from Irish Sea to North Sea

ISBN 978 1 84513 560 7

The Capital Ring
Colin Saunders

78 miles of green corridor encircling inner London

ISBN 978 1 84513 568 3

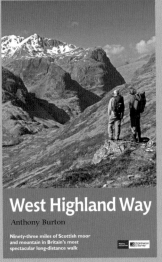

West Highland Way
Anthony Burton

Ninety-three miles of Scottish moor and mountain in Britain's most spectacular long-distance walk

ISBN 978 1 84513 569 0

Published by Aurum